Essays in Biography

Essays in Biography

Carl Rollyson

iUniverse, Inc.

New York Lincoln Shanghai

Essays in Biography

iUniverse books may be ordered through booksellers or by contacting:

iUniverse
2021 Pine Lake Road, Suite 100
Lincoln, NE 68512
www.iuniverse.com
1-800-Authors (1-800-288-4677)

ISBN: 0-595-34181-0

Printed in the United States of America

Contents

INTRODUCTION

The title of this book is a play on words. To essay is to make an attempt, a test, or a trial. By definition, the word suggests an effort that is less than definitive. In biography, no one can have the last word; there is always another possible interpretation of a life, another way of composing the biographical subject's story. Yet every day, students consult biographies in reference books that purport to provide a factual record of a person's life. Of course there are facts, but even the reference book biography is an interpretation, a narrative arrangement, a categorical assessment of a subject.

An essay in biography, then, is an effort to comprehend a life that is inherently incomplete and subject to revision. Which words the biographer chooses, which events he emphasizes, and the shape given to a subject's life, vary from one biographical account to another. Consult several reference books and see which details dominate the entry on the biographical subject.

Biography is by its very nature a contentious genre. I have provided a brief history of the genre that emphasizes how biographies have been censored because I want to emphasize that the genre is a form of knowledge that is constantly under attack. Many of the facts about a biographical subject's life that are blandly presented in reference books have been discovered by biographers at great cost to their reputations. With the history of biography as a censored genre in mind, I hope that readers of biography will look more critically at the biographies they read—no matter whether those biographies are book-length narratives or short encyclopedia entries.

As a biographer I have contributed many brief biographies to publications such as *Collier's Yearbook*, *American National Biography*, *The Encyclopedia of Southern Culture*, the *Great Lives* series, and to many other reference books. The essays have been formulaic in nature—that is, they have followed a structure mandated by the publisher. Even within these rigid restraints, however, my sensibility as a biographer is apparent. By bringing together this sampling of my work, I am attempting to review for myself and for other readers of biography, how the biographer's biases mesh with the conventions of biography as a genre.

I also intend for these essays—first published by Salem Press, which has generously allowed me to reprint them—to serve as a model for students of the genre to emulate and to modify. In doing so, I am attempting to prepare writers for the complex task of integrating a subject's life and work in the short compass of an essay. The biographical essay, I contend, is a unique form of knowledge. How we come to understand the work of Lillian Hellman or Rembrandt, for example, is inseparable from an understanding of their lives and their place in the history, literature, philosophy, and art.

I insist on this life-and-work approach even as modern critics contend that the life and work are separable—that knowledge of the artist's life is not needed to understand the artist's work. No one would make that kind of case for a political figure like Napoleon, but art has somehow become sacrosanct—at least for modernist critics. Of course, an appreciation of art is possible without knowing anything about the artist. But I find it baffling to suppose that this same art may not acquire another dimension when the artist's biography is known. Shakespeare is often cited as a weapon against the biographer. The poet Alfred Tennyson actually expressed his gratitude that we know so little about the world's greatest dramatist. Biography, Tennyson implies, just gets in the way of understanding art. But what would we not give to know more about Shakespeare? Why is it that literary critics such as Stephen Greenblatt feel compelled to write speculative biographies that attempt to make Shakespeare more of a man and not just a writer of plays? What would we not give to understand more of the process that resulted in the creation of Shakespeare's plays? This is the great appeal of films like *Shakespeare in Love.*

The truth is we cannot let Shakespeare alone; we want to know about how Shakespeare *became* Shakespeare. This desire for biography is universal: we want to know about the politician and his politics, the dancer and the dance, the critic and his criticism. The appetite for biography is insatiable. As I explain in a second essay, "Biography in the Marketplace," the genre has been a staple of the publishing industry and a favorite of readers since the 18th century. While modern scholars have shown considerable interest in why the novel became such a popular and influential genre, the same kind of attention has not been accorded to biography. Scholars produce biography, but they do not reflect much on its significance. Thus *Essays in Biography* is also an attempt to explore the nature of biography itself: why it is written, how it is written, and what happens to biography after it is published.

In some cases, I have tried to emulate Plutarch, the father of biography. The influence of his *Parallel Lives* is most apparent in my juxtaposition of essays on Leo Strauss and Hippolyte Taine, and on Winston Churchill and Napoleon

Bonaparte. Unlike Plutarch, I do not explicitly compare these pairs, but I enjoin the reader to do so.

PART ONE.

BIOGRAPHY: A BRIEF HISTORY OF A CENSORED GENRE

Biography as a literary genre is largely the product of the eighteenth century and of one seminal work, James Boswell's *Life of Samuel Johnson* (1791). Of course, biographies had appeared earlier, including several by Johnson himself, and the idea of biography extends backward to medieval saints' lives and to Plutarch (46?-120), whose *Parallel Lives* has exerted an enormous influence on the history of biography. But Boswell's innovations revolutionized the genre and made it the target of suppression and censorship. He sought not only to memorialize a great man but to reveal his flaws. Boswell reported long stretches of Johnson's conversation, noted his mannerisms, and in general gave an intimate picture such as no biographer had ever before dared to attempt.

Because Boswell was Johnson's friend, and because Johnson had sanctioned this minute attention to his life and believed in the superiority of biography as a genre, Boswell escaped becoming the target of censorship himself. But biographers since Boswell have had to confront numerous efforts to discourage, to censor, and even to ban, by legal action, the appearance of their books. Biographers themselves have colluded in censorship, and their subjects have often destroyed papers and mobilized friends and families to thwart the biographer's investigations.

Nineteenth-century biography

After Boswell, there was a retreat from his bolder innovations which amounted to self-censorship on the biographer's part. In his *Memoirs of the Life of Sir Walter Scott* (1837–1838), John Gibson Lockhart explicitly eschewed Boswell's intimate

1

focus. As Scott's son-in-law, Lockhart wanted to preserve both a relative's and a great man's dignity, and thus the biographer became, in Ian Hamilton's words, a "keeper of the flame," the one anointed to protect the hero's reputation.

Nineteenth-century biography is replete with examples of this self-censorship. Byron's biographer burned his subject's memoir lest it disgrace his subject. Henry James attempted to fix his own posthumous reputation by burning many of his papers and letters and writing fiction that denigrated the snooping biographer. Thomas Hardy tried to forestall biographers by writing his own but attributing it to the pen of his second wife, Florence Emily Hardy. Mrs. Gaskell, Charlotte Brontë's biographer, ruthlessly suppressed evidence that might show Brontë to be anything other than a conventional nineteenth-century woman. When Thomas Carlyle's biographer, James Anthony Froude, braved this trend against truth and allowed his subject's dark side to show, he was vilified in the press.

The preferred form of biography was not only sanitized, it allowed the biographer virtually no leeway to interpret his or her subject. Instead the biographer presented documents with a narrative that loosely linked them together and gave an account of the subject's times. These multi-volume life and times biographies encased their subjects in piety and euphemism.

Twentieth-century biography

In *Eminent Victorians* (1918), Lytton Strachey shattered the nineteenth-century tradition of reverence, censorship, and suppression. Instead of the lengthy tome, he wrote essays questioning the probity of public figures such as Cardinal Manning and General Gordon. He skewered his subjects by pointing to telling psychological details. Above all, he offered his own interpretations, eschewing long quotations from documents or any deference to authority other than his own.

After Strachey, the twentieth-century biographer has had to ask how much of a subject's private life should be told. No self-respecting biographer can merely cede control to the subject's friends and family. But a subject's papers and the right to quote from the subject's published and unpublished work still reside with families, friends, and literary estates. If a biographer wants full cooperation from them, he or she can seek "authorization." But authorization may require the biographer to adhere to a view of the subject pleasing to a literary executor. Executors can help biographers get publishing contracts; they can also threaten publishers, refuse to make material available to the biographer, and even sue the biographer and publisher over matters of libel, invasion of privacy, and copyright infringement. Even when no legal action is taken, a literary estate can poison the atmosphere in which biographers work—a fact well documented in Janet Malcolm's account of Sylvia Plath's biographers in *The Silent Woman*.

The modern way to censor or suppress an unauthorized biography is to carefully ration or withhold permission to quote from the biographical subject's published and unpublished work. The most famous case involves Ian Hamilton's biography of J.D. Salinger. When Hamilton sent Salinger a copy of his yet unpublished biography, Salinger took him to court alleging that Hamilton had infringed Salinger's copyright by quoting certain unpublished letters. In fact, Hamilton had quoted a very modest portion of those letters in accord with his understanding of what is deemed "fair use," a legal doctrine that allows writers to quote from published and unpublished work without securing permission to do so. The judgment against Salinger and his publisher Random House, which forced them to reset the book and eliminate all quotations from unpublished letters, had a chilling affect on the publishing industry. In one instance, Louise DeSalvo, author of an unauthorized controversial biography of novelist Virginia Woolf, was limited to quoting no more than 100 words from voluminous unpublished writings. Carl Rollyson, author of an unauthorized biography of journalist and novelist Martha Gellhorn, was threatened with legal action by Gellhorn, and his publisher allowed him to quote nothing from her unpublished papers. Biographers of other controversial figures, such as L. Ron Hubbard, founder of the Church of Scientology, were also taken to court. Margaret Walker, biographer of novelist Richard Wright, was sued for quoting from letters Wright sent to her. In these two cases, biographers prevailed in court and their books were not suppressed or censored. But the damage was already done, for it made publishers much more wary of publishing unauthorized biographies.

Censorship involving political figures has actually been much less prevalent because the law regards them as public figures, and it is much more difficult to sue biographers for invasion of privacy, libel, or copyright infringement. Powerful figures such as urban planner, Robert Moses, have tried to stop biographers, but the realm of the politician is so much larger and harder to control that aggressive unauthorized biographers such as Robert Caro have been able to acquire access to the essential evidence. Of course pressure can be brought to bear by powerful families. The Kennedys, for example, attacked William Manchester's biography of John F. Kennedy, making it difficult but not impossible for him to publish his book.

Recent court decisions and a Congressional amendment clarifying that fair use applies to unpublished as well as published work have eased the problem of censorship for biographers. But wherever a prominent person's papers are in the hands of an estate with the power to give or withhold permission to quote from published and unpublished work, the biographer may be in the position of negotiating the truth, of deciding what can be left in or out of a biography to satisfy the keepers of the flame.

Bibliography

Ian Hamilton, *Keepers of the Flame: Literary Estates and the Rise of Biography From Shakespeare to Plath* (Boston: Faber & Faber, 1992) and Michael Millgate, *Testamentary Acts: Browning, Tennyson, James Hardy* (New York: Oxford University Press, 1992) are the key works for studying censorship in biography and the biographer's relationship with literary estates. See also Ian Hamilton, *In Search of J.D. Salinger* (New York: Random House, 1988) and Janet Malcolm, *The Silent Woman* (New York: Knopf, 1994). Steve Weinberg, *Telling the Untold Story: How Investiage Reporters are Changing the Craft of Biography* (Columbia: University of Missouri Press, 1992), provides many examples of censorship in biography, including his own battle to publish a biography of magnate Armand Hammer.

PART TWO.

BIOGRAPHY IN THE MARKETPLACE

Since the eighteenth century, biography has been a staple of the publishing industry, and though fashions in publishing have changed, and biography itself has gone through various developments as a literary genre, it is remarkable how constant the market for biographies has been for nearly three hundred years. One reason for this extraordinary stability—at least in the English and American markets—is the premium that has been put on individual experience. Anglo-Americans have elevated individuality into a sacrosanct doctrine and have worried whenever they espied signs that it is under attack. John Stuart Mill fretted in the middle of the nineteenth century that the English were losing some of their vaunted eccentricity, and William Faulkner lamented in his mid-century novel, *Requiem for a Nun* (1951), that his region was becoming swallowed up in the uniformity of modern day mass society. Faulkner, at least, detected countervailing forces: the further people are removed from their origins and sense of identity, the stronger is their desire to recover them. His insight has surely been born out in the success of books and television programs that are, in essence, group biographies—best epitomized by Alex Haley's *Roots* and Ken Burns's *The Civil War*.

At the beginning of the book market for biographies, eighteenth century booksellers had to be convinced that biographies would sell as well as novels and histories—the mass and elite entertainments, respectively, of their day. Biography then, as today, could be made appealing if it focused on the famous and infamous, on heroes and scoundrels. As now, it was then the mode to write up the lives of criminals, adventurers, explorers, the shipwrecked and the disaster-prone. Robinson Crusoe, for example, had his real-life counterpart in Alexander Selkirk.

But biography could also draw upon a distinguished ancient author, Plutarch, and claim a moral purpose in narrating individual lives. Let it be remembered that Samuel Johnson, now such an august figure in the annals of biography, began as a hack busily writing up the lives of the renowned and notorious while arguing on behalf of biography as a literary form. On one occasion he conflated literary and commercial interests by writing an eloquent biography of a rogue, Richard Savage, who also happened to be a noteworthy minor poet Johnson had befriended.

It was the market that dictated what came to be known as Johnson's *Lives of the Poets*. A group of London booksellers persuaded him to write the acclaimed prefaces to poetry anthologies. Johnson drew on a lifetime of learning, conducted relatively little research, and wrote rapidly—like the glorious hack he was.

Biography, then, went hand-in-hand with the expanding capitalism of the eighteenth-century Anglo-American market. Then, as today, a poet or novelist—say Robert Southey, for example—would turn to biography, writing a life of Admiral Nelson the way Norman Mailer has done with Marilyn Monroe and his biography of Picasso. Curiously, Mailer has been accused of faults that could be equally detected in Johnson—slipshod research and tendentious conclusions. Yet in both cases, what makes their biographies popular—notwithstanding their defects—is not merely the sensationalism of their material but the liberties taken with the evidence, allowing them to propose creative insights into their subjects that are beyond the reach of more plodding and ostensibly more serious biographers, who are also less marketable.

Does the market, then, drive biography? To a large extent it does, though not quite in the simplistic way that the term market-driven implies. It is not the case that only the biographies publishers want get published. Or to be more precise, it is writers who make publishers want to publish certain biographies. Begin with what the trade publisher[1] needs: a biography that will sell. This almost surely means, one would suppose, a life of a well-known figure. True enough, but as soon as a biographer proposes a subject instantly recognizable to the public, the publisher is likely to say: "No, so and so has already been 'done.'" Professional biographers refute that objection by writing book proposals[2] that demonstrate how much new material is to be had, or how different their treatment of the subject will be from previous biographies. The publisher's attitude, in this instance,

---

1.   I say "trade publisher," meaning one that is concerned with turning a profit in the open marketplace, though increasingly university presses have turned to biography as a way of attracting a broader audience and significant profits.

has been a boon to biography, for it has made the contemporary biographer search sources diligently and innovatively and come to grips with style and structure.

Style and structure were precisely what nineteenth century biographies often lacked, when it was enough to write an idealized, bowdlerized, life-and-letters treatment of a subject that a Victorian public accepted, indeed craved, in a century that celebrated progress and prosperity. Without an aggressive market mentality such as is manifested by twentieth-century publishers, biography as a genre, with a few significant exceptions, languished in the nineteenth century, which turned it into a reliable, but staid form of literature.

Freud destroyed forever these Victorian panegyrics of the great by speculating boldly on the repressed sexuality of Leonardo and other great artists and leaders. He did not thereby destroy biography. On the contrary, individuality now became not a happy given—something one was born with and developed—but what one struggled to achieve and then maintain. The heroic battle became internalized, and the hero could be not only the soldier but the literary figure—the subject not merely of a biographical essay on the life and work, as in Johnson's day, but of the most penetrating, microscopic reading of personality that seemed—even if it promised more than it delivered—scientific in its rigor.

The reading public has responded well to this new biography, pioneered by Lytton Strachey in the 1920s, which, like Freud, refused to take its subject at face value. Biographies that attempt an intimate view of the subject are often accused of purveying gossip and of uncovering secrets for the sheer delight, as it were, of creating a scandal. Of course, there is truth in this criticism, but it misses the point. Contemporary biography is not merely hauling down its subjects to the level of its readers; it is making accessible precisely the process of self-formation that can only be glimpsed in minute particulars, in the gradual accumulation of experience that represents the modern self.

---

2.   The advent of the book proposal, fostered by the super agent, Scott Meredith, certainly aided biographers, in that the same proposal could be submitted to several publishers at once. Not only did this increase interest in biographies, it aided biographers by providing them with immediate feedback on their subjects—not merely on whether the subjects would sell but on how publishers, who are, after all, the author's first readers, reacted to the subject. How intrinsically interesting was the subject? How would a general audience be likely to react to the biography? And since proposals traditionally contain a section on "the competition," the biographer was also forced to take a hard look at what had already been done on his or her subject—not necessarily the first thing a biographer would otherwise do.

Publishers have abetted biographers more than the critics and the academy[3] because they have been so open to multiple treatments of the same subjects. Though a publisher may be skeptical at first, a well researched and written proposal on a familiar subject will often be bought, even as reviewers groan that they must read yet another biography of Napoleon or Lincoln or Marilyn Monroe. Certainly there can be a glut of biographies on a particular subject, but in the main several biographies on the same subject teach that the same life can be read in many different ways, depending on the nature of the available evidence (which changes as new discoveries are made and restrictions are lifted from research collections) and of the biographer. And it is not certain that there would be as wide a field for biographers were it not for the demands of the market seeking novelty and new ways of telling old stories.

It is also true that a biography of an obscure figure, or of a slighted subject deserving of major treatment, may excite a publisher because of the quality of the biographer's writing—although publishers do seem increasingly conservative and unwilling to take risks on unknowns. Happily, university presses are beginning to publish more biographies, sometimes filling the gap opened up by trade publishers who see no profit, or not enough profit, in certain kinds of biography. Bryan Boyd's biography of Vladimir Nabokov is a case in point. His contract with Simon and Schuster was cancelled as soon as the publisher learned that Boyd insisted on dividing his work into two volumes. In most cases, multiple volume biographies are not a good financial investment for the largest trade houses, since after the first volume is published sales drop significantly—even for such acclaimed work as Michael Holroyd's volumes on George Bernard Shaw. Boyd was fortunate not only to have Princeton University Press publish his biography

---

3. It is remarkable how little interest scholars have shown in biography—either as a literary form or as an important element of popular culture. In recent years, this has been somewhat rectified with studies of the history of biography, and with scholarly biographers writing books and essays on the theory and practice of biography. Nevertheless, compared with the incredible volume of work on the novel, for example, biography has clearly been slighted. It can be argued, of course, that as a genre biography has not produced the range of first-rate work found in the novel, but from an historical point of view, given the undeniable importance of biography in shaping literary opinion and in establishing a canon of great writers, the academy has been remiss both in neglecting the merits of biography per se and in failing to recognize how, practically speaking, biography has contributed to the development of literature itself.

in two volumes, but to make it a lead title, which enjoyed large sales by university press standards.

Similarly, university presses have sometimes acquired titles from trade houses, for paperback publication. The University of Tennessee Press, for example, has published in paperback Ann Waldron's fine biography of Caroline Gordon, and the University of Massachusetts Press will publish in paperback Ann Hulbert's acclaimed biography of Jean Stafford. Such titles will appeal to a broad literary audience while also satisfying the scholarly mission of university presses.

That university presses did not publish more biography in the past is largely due to fashions in the academy. For years the "New Criticism" taught that there was virtually no value in studying an author's life, that the work of art must be discussed only in its own terms, and that it was illegitimate to bootleg biography, so to speak, into legitimate literary criticism. More recently, the deconstructionists have attacked the very notion of an author and have been, for the most part, hostile to biography.

It is difficult to predict the future of biography in publishing. Based on current trends, biographers of certain subjects without mass appeal will have to turn to university or small presses, but these alternatives to trade publishing have sometimes been able to produce best sellers and have their own impact on the market for biography. A small press may understand how to target a biography for a specific audience and will rely on the chain bookstores and websites much less than trade publishers. And independent bookstores have often been instrumental in promoting non-trade titles. On balance, publishers' continued willingness to consider biography from virtually every kind of writer—from the journalist to the academic to the novelist and so on—bodes well for the genre. It has been said, sometimes with scorn, that anyone can write a biography—perhaps because in the lowly estimation of some, all that is required is to collect and arrange the facts. For the health of biography in the marketplace, however, the idea that one can not only read, but perhaps also write a good biography has always served as the best tonic for the form, a tonic publishers have always been willing to patent and to distribute to the widest possible audience.

PART THREE.

BIOGRAPHICAL ESSAYS

BIOGRAPHERS

Plutarch (c. 46 A.D.–120 A.D.)

Plutarch is the greatest biographer of antiquity who taught his successors how to combine depth of psychological and moral insight with a strong narrative that evokes the greatness and excitement of his subjects' lives.

Most of Plutarch's writing was not accomplished until late middle age. He was born in a Roman province to an old and wealthy Greek family. He received a comprehensive education in Athens, where he studied rhetoric, physics, mathematics, medicine, the natural sciences, philosophy, and Greek and Latin writing. His world view was strongly influenced by Plato (c.427–347 B.C.), and he took considerable interest in theology, serving as the head priest at Delphi in the last twenty years of his life. By the time he was twenty, he had rounded out his education by traveling throughout Greece, Asia Minor, and Egypt.

Before his writing career began, Plutarch worked in Chaeronea as a teacher and was its official representative to the Roman governor. Later he undertook diplomatic trips to Rome, where he befriended several important public servants. The prestige of Greek learning stood very high in the Roman Empire, and Plutarch eventually was invited to lecture in various parts of Italy on moral and philosophical subjects. Sometime in his late thirties, he began to organize his notes into essays. There is evidence to suggest that by the time he was forty, Plutarch enjoyed a highly receptive audience for his lectures. For this was a time in which the Roman emperors were particularly favorable to Greek influences.

Although Plutarch could easily have made a career of his Roman lecture tours, he returned to his home in Chaeronea at about the age of fifty. There he served in many administrative posts with the evident intention of reviving Greek culture and religion. His principal great work, *Parallel Lives*, was written in these years when his sense of civic responsibility and leadership had matured, and when he was able to draw on his considerable experience of political power.

In *Parallel Lives*, Plutarch chose to write about actual historical figures. The lives were parallel in the sense that he paired his subjects, so that Alexander and Julius Caesar, Demosthenes and Cicero, could be written about in terms of each other. It was important to have a basis of comparison, to show how equally famous men had arrived at their achievements in similar and different circumstances, with personalities that could be contrasted and balanced against each other. For Plutarch's aim was not merely to describe lives but to judge them, to weigh their ethical value and to measure their political effectiveness. Clearly, he believed that human beings learned by example. So he would present exemplary lives, complete with his subjects' strengths and weaknesses, in order to provide a comprehensive view of the costs and the benefits of human accomplishment.

Plutarch has often been attacked for being a poor historian. What this means is that sometimes he gets his facts wrong. On occasion he is so interested in making a moral point, in teaching a lesson, that he ruins the particularity and complexity of an individual life. He has also been guilty of relying on suspect sources, of taking reports at face value because they fit preconceived notion of his subject.

While these faults must be acknowledged and compensated for, they should not be allowed to obscure the enormous value of Plutarch's biographies. In the first place, he realized he was not writing histories but lives, and that some of his sources were questionable. Unlike the historian, he was not primarily interested in the events of the past. On the contrary, it was the personalities of his subjects that had enduring value for him. To Plutarch, there was a kind of knowledge of human beings that could not be found in the close study of events or in the narration of historical epochs. As he puts it, "a slight thing like a phrase or a jest often makes a greater revelation of character than battles where thousands fall, or the greatest armaments, or sieges of cities." Plutarch found his evidence in the seemingly trifling anecdotes about great personages. He was of the conviction that an intense scrutiny of the individual's private as well as public behavior would yield truths about human beings not commonly found in histories.

Plutarch thought of himself as an artist. He was building portraits of his subjects: "just as painters get the likenesses in their portraits from the face and the expression of the eyes, wherein the character shows itself, but make very little account of the other parts of the body, so I must be permitted to devote myself rather to the signs of the soul in men, and by means of these to portray the life of each, leaving to others the description of their great contests."

As the founder of biography, Plutarch was pursuing psychological insight. Individuals were the expressions of a society, the eyes and face of the community, so to speak. He would leave to historians the description of society, "the other parts of the body."

What makes Plutarch convincing to this day is that he is loaded with perception. No biographer has surpassed him in summing up the essence of a life—perhaps because no modern biographer has believed so intensely as Plutarch did in "the soul in men." Each line in Plutarch's best biographical essays carries the weight and significance of a whole life. It is his ability to make his readers believe that he is imagining, say, Caesar's life from the inside, from Caesar's point of view, that makes the biographer such an attractive source that Shakespeare and many other great authors freely borrowed from him.

It has often been said that no biographer can truly penetrate his or her subject's mind. But Plutarch perfected a way of reading external events, of shaping them into a convincing pattern, until—like a great painting—his prose seems to emit the personality of his subject. Here, for example, is his account of Caesar's ambition:

> Caesar's successes…did not divert his natural spirit of enterprise and ambition to the enjoyment of what he had laboriously achieved, but served as fuel and incentive for future achievements, and begat in him plans for greater deeds and a passion for fresh glory, as though he had used up what he already had. What he felt was therefore nothing else than emulation of himself, as if he had been another man, and a sort of rivalry between what he had done and what he purposed to do

These two long sentences, with their complex clauses, are imitative of Caesar's life itself, for they demonstrate how ambition drove him on—not satisfying him but actually stimulating more exploits. Here was a great man who had set such a high example for himself that his life had turned into a competition with itself. Plutarch manages the uncanny feat of having Caesar looking at himself and thereby gives his readers the sensation of momentarily occupying Caesar's mind.

Plutarch was by no means interested only in men of great political and military accomplishment. His pairing of Demosthenes and Cicero, for example, is his way of paying respect to mental agility and the power of the word. Both men prepared for their public careers as orators through long careful training, but their personalities were quite different. Cicero was given to extraordinary boasting about himself whereas Demosthenes rarely spoke in his own favor. If Cicero was sometimes undone by his penchant for joking, there was nevertheless a pleasantness in him almost entirely lacking in Demosthenes. That two such different men should have parallel careers is surely part of Plutarch's point. There is no single pathway in life to success or failure, and personal faults—far from being extraneous—may determine the fate of a career. Shakespeare realized as much when he based much of his *Coriolanus* upon Plutarch's interpretation of the Roman leader's choleric character and his devotion to his mother.

Most of *Parallel Lives* seems to have been written in the last twenty years of Plutarch's life—precisely at that point when he was most seriously occupied as a religious official, statesman, and diplomat. His studies of philosophy and religion surely gave him the confidence to assess the lives he would have his readers learn from.

Plutarch died an old man in peaceful repose recognized for his good services by his fellow Boethians who dedicated an inscription to him at Delphi.

As it is suggested in *The Oxford Classical Dictionary*, Second Edition, Plutarch was most concerned with the education of his heroes, whose stories proceeded from their family background, education, entrance into the larger world, climax of achievement, and their fame and fortune (good and bad). He exerted a profound influence on the Roman world of his time, on the Middle Ages, and on a group of important writers—chiefly Montaigne (1533–1592), Shakespeare (1564–1616), Dryden (1631–1700), and Rousseau (1712–1778). If his impact is less obvious in modern times, it is probably because there is less confidence in the moral patterns Plutarch boldly delineated. What biographer today can speak, as Plutarch did, to the whole educated world, knowing that he had behind him the prestige and the grandeur of Greek literature and religion?

Bibliography

Barrow, R. H. *Plutarch and His Times*. Bloomington: Indiana University Press, 1967. Includes map of central Greece. Emphasizes Plutarch's Greek background, with chapters on his role as a teacher and his relationship to the Roman Empire. The bibliography is divided between English and foreign titles.

Gianakaris, C. J. *Plutarch*. New York: Twayne Publishers, 1970. One of the best short introductions to Plutarch. Includes detailed chronology, discussions of all of Plutarch's important works, a selected and annotated bibliography, and a useful index. Gianakaris writes with a firm grasp of the scholarship on Plutarch, corrects errors of earlier writers, and conveys great enthusiasm for his subject.

Jones, C. P. Plutarch and Rome. London: Oxford University Press, 1971. Several chapters on Plutarch's career, on his lives of the Caesars, and on the sources, methods, and purposes of *Parallel Lives*. Concentrates on the importance of Rome in Plutarch's life and work. Extensive bibliography of books and articles with a helpful chronological table

Russell, D. A. *Plutarch*. London: Duckworth, 1973. Draws on the best English and French scholarship. Slightly more difficult than Gianakaris as an introduction. Chapters on language, style, and form, on the philosopher and his religion, and on Plutarch and Shakespeare. Several appendices including one on editions and translations. A general bibliography and index

Shackford, Martha Hale. *Plutarch in Renaissance English with Special Reference to Shakespeare*. Wellesley College, 1929. The scholarly monograph contains a sketch of Plutarch's life, chapters on his influence in the Middle Ages, the Italian Renaissance, and the English Renaissance. Particularly interesting for its discussion of Plutarch's impact on English poets such as Sir Phillip Sidney. A long chapter on Plutarch as a source and influence on Shakespeare.

Wardman, Alan. *Plutarch's Lives*. Berkeley: University of California Press, 1974. A very detailed scholarly discussion of *Parallel Lives*. Chapter on "History: Some Problems of Method." The bibliography includes many foreign titles, especially from French scholarship.

Leon Edel (1907–1997)

Biographies: *Henry James. The Untried Years: 1843–1870* (1953); *Henry James. The Conquest of London: 1870–1881* (1962); *Henry James. The Middle Years: 1882–1895* (1962); *Henry James. The Treacherous Years: 1895–1901* (1969); *Henry James. The Master: 1901–1916 (1972); The Life of Henry James, Volume 1, Volume 2,* (revised edition 1977); *Henry James: A Life* (condensed and revised edition, 1985); *Bloomsbury: A House of Lions* (1979); *Stuff of Sleep and Dreams* (1982); *Writing Lives: Principia Biographica* (1984).

Leon Edel's concern with the psychological interpretation of lives is reflected not only in his biographies but in his critical study, *The Psychological Novel* (1955). He is regarded as one of the foremost literary biographers of the twentieth century. He has earned his reputation through his innovative multi-volume biography of Henry James and his persuasive arguments over many years for a sophisticated biographical method. He has been an ardent advocate for applying the insights of modern psychology to the study of literature and of writers' lives. No critical account of modern biographical writing would be complete without a discussion of Edel's theory and practice of literary biography. Recent studies and collections of essays on the nature of biography contain contributions by him or about his impact on what he calls the writing of lives.

Leon Edel was born on September 9, 1907, in Pittsburgh, Pennsylvania. In 1927 and 1928, he received his BA and MA degrees from McGill University in Montreal, Canada. In 1932, he received a Docteur es Lettres degree from the University of Paris. He served with the United States Army in France and Germany (1943–1947) and was decorated with the Bronze Star Medal. He was also Chief of Information Control, News Agency, in the United States Zone in 1946–1947.

Edel's academic career began in 1932 as an assistant professor at Sir George Williams College in Montreal, but after two years he turned to a career as a journalist (1934–1943). After his years in the army, he assumed a series of distinguished academic positions at Princeton University (1951–1952), New York University (1952–1972), Indiana University (1954), University of Hawaii (1955, 1969), Harvard University (1959–1960), Purdue University (1970), and Dartmouth University (1977).

Edel was the recipient of major academic and literary awards, including a Guggenheim Fellowship (1936–1938, 1965–1966), and a Bollingen Fellowship (1959–1961). In addition to numerous honorary degrees, he was awarded several distinguished literary prizes: the National Institute of Arts and Letters Award, 1959; the National Book Award for nonfiction, 1963; the Pulitzer Prize for biography, 1963; the National Arts Club Medal for Literature, 1981, and others.

Throughout his career as a biographer and as a biographical theorist, Leon Edel maintained that biographers must strive for excellence of literary form. A fine biography must have a pleasing aesthetic shape, a concrete delineation of human character, and an economical approach to the biographical subject that reveal the most telling details of a life. In short, modern literary biography must model itself after the novel in order to achieve a vivid and deeply penetrating study of the subject's life.

The biographer should aspire to be an artist, Edel insists. What is most important is that the "central myth" of the writer's life is revealed. Edel's contention is that there is a unified shaping vision by which the creative artist lived, and the biographer must discover and dramatize that vision.

As a literary critic, Edel has shown that the themes of a writer's life and writing are inevitably intertwined. This does not mean that all creative work is autobiographical, but it does mean, according to Edel, that all art arises from deeply personal feelings: "We know that all literature is a form of disguise, a mask, a fable, a mystery: and behind the mask is the author," he writes in the foreword to *Stuff of Sleep and Dreams*.

Edel's theory of literary biography is best understood by citing an example from his work on Henry James. In his condensed and revised version of the biography (1985), Edel provides a remarkably succinct and insightful summary of one of James's finest and most intricate novels, *The Ambassadors* (1903) that at the same time is a profound revelation of James's own psyche. The novel is told from the point of view of Lambert Strether—in Edel's words, "a middle-aged 'ambassador sent out" to Europe to retrieve a young American male who has apparently been seduced by the old world charms of a mature woman. The novel is as much about Strether's acculturation as it is about the young man's presumed debauchery. Edel focuses on two key scenes that reveal Strether's developing realization that in Europe the young man has had the opportunity to grow and to fulfill himself. Concomitantly, Strether recognizes that he has not himself managed to live life to the full. Insulated from the choices Europe has offered this young man, Strether has to admit he has never pursued his own desires or developed his own talents. In sum, he has never been free, and his decision is to allow this young—in many ways Strether's younger self—the liberty to choose his own life. At the conclusion of his remarks on *The Ambassadors*, Edel notes that "beyond 'technique' and its resourceful experiments, beyond its neat symmetrical design, the care with which it is composed'...[the novel] spoke for the central myth of Henry James's life." That myth has to do with leaving America as a young man for the richer life of Europe—not an easy choice for James who had to struggle with what Edel calls the "authority figures" of his Puritan past. James, in other words, had to reverse the very direction of his family history—the movement from Europe to America—and contend that a return to Europe was, in fact, a liberating decision. All of the terror, the uncertainty, and the anguish, but also the charm, the boldness, and the creativity of James's commitment to a life in Europe are dramatized in the character of Lambert Strether.

Edel's own artistry as a biographer is revealed in his emphasis on the word "composed" to speak for both James's novel and his life. The novel is not autobiography in the sense of reproducing the events of James's life, but it is his life in the most profound, psychological sense.

In all of his writing on biographical theory, Edel was careful to point out that he was not psychoanalyzing the writer; that is, Edel was not claiming to know James's innermost thoughts, or to be engaging in a scientific analyses of the writer's maladies. Edel was no doctrinaire follower of Sigmund Freud, the founder of modern psychoanalysis. But Edel is impressed with Freud's analyses of the patterns of people's lives and of those crucial moments in which truths about their lives are revealed.

In *Stuff of Sleep and Dreams*, Edel defines his terms. He favors the phrase "literary psychology" to distinguish his method from "other psychologies that are concerned with treating neuroses and pathological conditions of mental health. In other words, literary psychology is criticism and biography divorced from psychotherapy." In the same book, in a chapter entitled "The Nature of Psychological Evidence," Edel enumerates the "three postulates" he has taken from psychoanalysis. He believes there is such a thing as the unconscious that manifests itself in human behavior, "in dreams, in imaginings, thoughts." Within this unconscious are "certain suppressed feelings and states of being which sometimes emerge into awareness in the consciously created forms of literature." Finally, "by the process of induction—that is, by examining the mental representation in words of things not present to the senses—we can detect deeper intentions and meanings, valuable both to the biographer and the critic."

Edel insists that the biographer works with facts and with evidence. His biography of James is the distillation of a massive amount of material on the writer's life and work that includes diaries, journals, notebooks, letters, and various accounts of James's life by himself and by others. As Edel often said, the biographer is not free to imagine facts, but he is charged with inventing a form that makes the most profound sense of his subject's life.

It was perhaps inevitable with a great writer like James, who lived a long, productive life, and whose archive continues to grow with newly discovered letters and many other materials, that Edel was forced to write a lengthy, multi-volume biography.

Nevertheless, the size of the James biography would seem to contradict Edel's strictures about precision and economy in the writing of lives. Edel tacitly acknowledged this discrepancy between his theory and practice by revising and rewriting his biography twice—in two volumes in 1977, and then in one volume in 1985. Each time he did more than cut wordage; he added newly discovered material and (with the aid of editors) reshaped the entire biography.

In the last edition of the James biography, Edel also responded to "the changes that have occurred in biographical writing and in social attitudes toward privacy and our sexual lives." It is not that he has gone in search of James's "sex life," Edel points out, but rather that he has abandoned "former reticences" and "proprieties" of an earlier age. He also acknowledges the fact that his earlier edition of the biography was written "out of respect for surviving members of the James family, the children of William James."

All of these changes that occurred over more than three decades in Edel's work on Henry James make a fascinating study of how the writing and the discussion of biography have changed. Edel is one of several biographers who have taken bolder positions as literary writers—not just as compilers of facts. Edel has led the way in speculating on the pattern of James's life and in refusing to be bound by conventions other biographers have treated as sacrosanct. For example, although his life of James is told in chronological fashion, he has availed himself of novelistic devices—such as the flashback and flash-forward to earlier and later events in James's life. The implication of such techniques is that "the facts do not speak for themselves," that the biographer must be an interpreter of his evidence and create a structure for it.

While Edel has enormous prestige as a biographer, he has not been immune from criticism. He has been accused of adopting the theories of modern psychology too readily and of shifting the emphasis in biography too far toward forms of literature like the novel. Other theorists of biography have insisted on a strictly chronological approach to biography and have eschewed the use of psychological theory, since the employment of fictional techniques and of psychological speculation reveal, in their view, more about the biographer than the subject of the biography. In the main, however, Edel has remained the principal theorist of biography whose arguments have been open to challenge but not to significant refutation.

In *Writing Lives*, Edel discussed many of his fellow biographers, especially predecessors like Lytton Strachey (1880–1932) and Andre Maurois (1885–1967). His chief criticism of them is their tendency to allow their own personalities to distort the lives they have written about. In a way, Edel's studies of his precursors constitute a reply to his critics. By studying how Strachey, Maurois, and others have been err to this tendency, Edel is critiquing his own practice. The single most important influence on Edel has surely been Strachey. In *Eminent Victorians*(1918), Strachey wrote pithy and provocative studies of Thomas Arnold, Florence Nightingale, General Gordon, and Cardinal Manning in order to debunk their "eminence." At the same time, Strachey was hailed as an artist for his turns of phrase, his economical use of biographical evidence, and his ability to dramatize human personality and history in essay-length form. Edel has not adopted Strachey's satirical style, but he has emulated Strachey's compression of human lives into deft, self-sufficient essays of human character.

Indeed, all of Edel's work after the James biography, including his study of the Bloomsbury group, has been predicated on the essay form. In this way, he has sought to vindicate his view that biography should be to the point; it should be the crystallization of a life, not a long and tedious—if faithful—chronicle of it.

W. A. Swanberg (1907–)

Biographies: *Jim Fisk: The Career of an Improbable Rascal* (New York: Scribner's, 1959); *Citizen Hearst* (New York: Scribner's, 1961); *Dreiser* (New York: Scribner's, 1965); *Pulitzer* (New York: Scribner's, 1967); *The Rector and the Rogue* (New York: Scribner's, 1969); *Luce and His Empire* (New York: Scribner's, 1972); *Norman Thomas: The Last Idealist* (New York: Scribner's, 1976); *Whitney Father, Whitney Heiress* (New York: Scribner's, 1980).

William Andrew Swanberg is best known for his biographies of William Randolph Hearst, Joseph Pulitzer, and Henry Luce, three titans of the newspaper and magazine publishing world. Swanberg's sole biography of a literary figure, Theodore Dreiser, might be viewed as an exception to his customary subject. Yet the biographer presents Dreiser's life in a way that is congruent with his other biographies and that raises significant questions about the practice of literary biography.

Swanberg was born in St. Paul, Minnesota, the son of Charles Henning and Valborg (Larsen) Swanberg, and attended the University of Minnesota, where he received his B.A. in 1930 and took graduate courses in 1931. After a miscellaneous series of jobs, he became assistant editor at Dell Publishing Company in New York City in 1936 and married Dorothy Upham Green. They have two children: John William and Sara Valborg. Swanberg was promoted to editor in 1936 and stayed at Dell until 1944, when he served as a writer in Europe for the U.S. Office of War Information. Since 1945, he has been a free-lance writer, with his career as a published biographer beginning in 1959 with a study of Jim Fisk.

Swanberg's second biography, *Citizen Hearst*, made his reputation as a fair, scrupulous, and engaging writer of famous, controversial lives. In a sense, all of Swanberg's biographies have been literary, for he has striven for a clean narrative line and fully realized characters. He likes to tell a story with carefully crafted chapter titles. Thus Book One of *Citizen Hearst* is entitled "The Prodigy," and its chapters bear such titles as "A Roughneck in Love," "Bless His Little Heart," and "Willie at Large." Such titles are never merely cute, although they are obviously designed to entice the reader and to establish the quick pace that is characteristic of good popular fiction. If Swanberg has not been criticized for such gimmicks, it is because he carefully documents his subjects and because his material is, in itself, colorful. William Randolph Hearst's father, for example, was quite literally a "roughneck in love," a crude frontier specimen who settled down to marriage with a genteel wife, so that the chapter title is no mere embellishment or exaggeration of Swanberg's sources.

What astonished many reviewers of *Citizen Hearst* was the depth of the biographer's sympathy for his subject. Hearst had been a much vilified figure in other biographies and treated as a figure of some menace in the film, *Citizen Kane*. While not minimizing Hearst's arrogance of power, Swanberg gives a complex, sophisticated view of a man who was raised to regard himself as a genius and as a law unto himself. So thoroughly drenched is the biographer in his sources that the reader imagines he has captured precisely the tone of life as rambunctious "Willie" himself must have experienced it. Swanberg neither excuses Hearst's excesses nor accuses him of wrongdoing. Rather the subject is presented much in the way Dreiser depicts his tycoon, Frank Cowperwood, with enormous empathy for a man of towering energy and ambition. Swanberg's prose, however, is circumspect, and he does not abandon himself to Dreiserian flourishes or apostrophes to the fates. The decorum of a biography, the recitation of the facts, is always paramount for Swanberg. A solid if not a brilliant stylist, he uses unadorned prose that appears to be a seamless part of the facts he presents. Language in his biographies rarely calls attention to itself, for to do so would surely raise questions about biographical interpretation and about the biographer's manipulation of his materials.

Swanberg rarely speculates. Very few of his sentences are prefaced with "perhaps" or "maybe" or qualified by "must have." A skilled researcher, he relies on his data and shapes a story from it. He does not ponder over the things he does not know. Occasionally, he will allow himself to present a version of what one of his subjects might have felt in a certain situation, but this is usually long after he has established his subject's character and a pattern of reactions that make the biographer's conjecture unobtrusive and even welcome. For example, after enumerating several instances of Dreiser's foolishness, after presenting in riveting detail the great middle-aged author's reckless passion for a young girl, Swanberg concludes: "He had been defeated at every turn. He had lost home, wife, Honeypot [Thelma Cudlipp], job, income, prestige and his splendid green-and-bronze office, and in the bargain he must have realized that he looked silly." There is not a shred of tangible evidence indicating how Dreiser felt, but given the circumstances and everything the reader knows up to this point about him, the biographer has earned the right to characterize his subject's feelings. Another biographer might be silent on this point, but at the risk of depriving his biography of emotional weight and insight.

As a personality, it is not surprising that Dreiser attracted Swanberg, for he had the same outsize protean appeal that distinguished Hearst. The two men were contemporaries who outraged society by thwarting its conventional codes.

They were also paradoxical figures who wanted to make an impression on their times, to be popular, and to create publications that would extend their influence. Dreiser was for a period an enormously successful magazine editor and throughout his life was lured into commercial schemes—like the creation of a motion picture company—that gave the lie to his anti-society side. Unlike many other literary figures Swanberg could have chosen, Dreiser has a kind of bulk, a massiveness that puts him in the same league as Hearst or Luce. Their craving for political and economic power is exactly what Dreiser found attractive, especially in his Cowperwood novels.

To write a biography of a literary figure, however, might have given trouble to a biographer with Swanberg's background. How to deal with the specifically literary aspects of Dreiser's life? Analysis of works of literature would have forced him into a method considerably different from his previous biographies. In part, at least, he would have to become a literary critic. And what would happen to his strong sense of narrative? Would it bog down in chapters of plot summary and interpretation, with the biographer having to conscientiously plod through both the atrocious books and the good ones? To what extent would his subject's books, some of them autobiographical, tend to usurp Swanberg's own narrative? How to prevent the reader from getting mired in detailed commentary on what was true and what was not in Dreiser's memoirs?

In the Author's Note and Acknowledgments, Swanberg indicates how he answered these questions:

> This book is intended solely as biography, not criticism. There have been many analyses of Dreiser's works, but no attempt to study the whole man. Not even during his busiest writing years was he exclusively a writer, being always a self-taught philosopher with strong views about society. He collided repeatedly with American culture, religion and politics. For a quarter-century he waged a violent battle against the censorship of art, and his works, if not his words, had a large share in the victory. Indeed, Dreiser was a fighter incarnate, always battling something, his compulsion toward social criticism and mystic philosophy so overmastered him that he all but abandoned creative writing. If his prejudices and contradictions were awesome, the mature Dreiser represents in extreme enlargement the confusions of the era after 1929 when intellectuals everywhere sought a better society, and when thinkers more competent than he proved as mistaken as he. But Dreiser was, in the extreme sense, an original. There has been no one like him. He deserves study simply as one of the most incredible of human beings, a man whose enormous gifts warred endlessly with grievous flaws.

For many literary biographers, a subject's written work is, in the main, the life, and the point is to show how the work and the life are of a piece. Swanberg suggests that Dreiser's writing can be treated separately—indeed it is so treated in numerous works of literary criticism that do not deal with the "whole man." But how, a literary biographer might ask, can there be a "whole man" in a biography that does not interpret the subject's writing? To say that there were periods when Dreiser did not write does not seem a very convincing argument, since all authors—even the most prolific—have periods when they do not write. Other authors have been just as involved in the political and social issues of their age and yet have also created unique personalities for themselves that surely are located, in important ways, in their writing. Why should Dreiser be any different? A literary biographer or critic might suspect that Swanberg has simply ducked the issue of literary biography altogether.

In his review of *Dreiser* (*New York Times Book Review*, May 16, 1965, p. 4), Robert E. Spiller suggests that a narrative of the subject's life is not enough, that somehow Swanberg has missed the heart of Dreiser by not dealing directly with his writing. Spiller does not fault Swanberg so much as suggest that biographical narrative cannot explain the creative personality: "[Swanberg's] theory is that if we can get an accurate account of all the events and people in Dreiser's life and know what happened to him at every stage, somehow we will have gone a long way toward accounting also for his novels, short stories, poems, plays, sketches."

Jason Epstein, on the other hand, writing in *The New York Review of Books* (June 3, 1965, p. 11) praises Swanberg for not writing "a novelist's literary life, that often wearisome genre, with its dutiful summaries of plot and character and neat packets of themes and symbols tossed in to give the whole a savor of textbook serviceability. But by concentrating on biographical data, Mr. Swanberg has done much to elucidate the art of the man who wrote *Sister Carrie* and *An American Tragedy*."

These two reactions to *Dreiser* are not so much opposed as they are divided in their judgment as to where the emphasis should be placed. Spiller focuses on what Swanberg has not been able to reveal given his methodology; Epstein concentrates on the virtues of the biographer's technique, admiring how much Swanberg has accomplished while implying in a phrase like "done much to elucidate" that not all has been divulged.

Both reviewers know Dreiser's writing. Spiller would like to see more interaction between that writing and the biographical narrative. Epstein is content, indeed pleased, with Swanberg's descriptions of the real-life models for Dreiser's fictional characters, with the "fascinating things" he learns about "those living creatures of Dreiser's literary production. We learn that Thelma Cudlipp, whose youthful fascination ended Dreiser's career as an editor, but also embellished the portrait of Cowperwood's mistress in *The Titan,* married extremely well and years later took up a decorous friendship with Dreiser after her mother had committed suicide. (Dreiser had portrayed Mrs. Cudlipp, who had broken up the affair, as a high-class madam).

Epstein takes pleasure in making his own connections between the life and the work by drawing on the "data" the biographer has presented. Spiller, on the other hand, would just as soon see the biographer perform some of this work. Epstein does, however, fault Swanberg for making "too little biographical use of Dreiser's fiction," especially during his middle years "when the exciting story is Dreiser's subterranean method of book planning and writing, not the parties Dreiser attended, his quarrels with publishers, or his fights with censors." In other words, there are parts of the biography where Swanberg's external approach, which allows the pattern of his subject's actions to make the case for his internal feelings, is successful; and there are other parts where only a foray into the subject's prose itself will yield the biographical truth.

While there may be this uneven quality in the biography's structure, it is also important to recognize that the strengths and weaknesses of Swanberg's method are also apparent line by line, so to speak, as he characterizes Dreiser's life and writing without actually providing the reader with a feel for how the writing succeeds or fails. Take, for example, Swanberg's treatment of *Sister Carrie*. Readers familiar with the novel would surely chafe at a plot summary, and Swanberg wisely does not provide one. Instead he tends to allude to Carrie's story, to Hurstwood's flight with the $10,000 from a safe, and to other events in the novel which only have a resonance for the reader of the biography if he or she has read *Sister Carrie*. It would have been possible to quote a few passages from the novel in order to render Dreiser's deep feelings without having to play the critic, which Swanberg is loathe to do. This would seem especially apposite since the biographer does manage to make a story out of Dreiser's composition of the novel, pointing out—in one instance—how the novelist "got stuck, unable to hit on a satisfactory way for Hurstwood to steal the money from the safe" and solved his dilemma by having him remove the money as the safe accidentally closes and locks. This is such a good scene in *Sister Carrie* that it is curious Swanberg does not quote a few sentences just to heighten his reader's interest in the deftness of Dreiser's writing.

It is as though Swanberg did not want to remind the reader of what it means to examine a literary text, to submerse oneself in the writer's style. The advantage for Swanberg is that there is no discrepancy between his words and Dreiser's. The whole story gets told in Swanberg's prose, and he thereby avoids the problem most literary biographies face: the extent to which the literary figure's writing is central to the text of the biography. By not quoting Dreiser, Swanberg has eliminated the problem of transitions from the subject's language to his own. Every aspect of the biography becomes subsumed in the biographer's language. As a tactical maneuver, Swanberg's choice is unassailable, since literary biographies—even the very best—get a wide range of reviews complaining that not enough or too much attention has been paid to the subject's writing. To claim that biography of the "whole man" is separable from the issue of his work is to dispatch a perennial problem of literary biography.

When Dreiser is divorced from his words, Swanberg is free to reconstitute and to dramatize his subject's life without competition from the very text (*Sister Carrie*) on which the biographer actually relies. The impact of the biographer's prose then becomes paramount. It is as if the only way Swanberg can tell the story of Dreiser's creation of *Sister Carrie* is to collect and concentrate his biographical data in passages that are the culmination of the biographer's research, and not of his subject's work:

> In *Carrie* for the first time of importance, Dreiser translated his own experience into the desperate, hopeless yearnings of his characters. *Ev'ry Month* [the magazine he edited] had held him in a tight little strait-jacket. His magazine articles were pot-boilers conforming to editors' wishes. Now the reluctant conformist was free to write as he pleased about life as he saw it. He let himself go far, far into unconformity, apparently not realizing the extent of his divagation, but surely there was unconscious rebellion against the restraints that had curbed him for four years. Although he had read Hardy with admiration and he was not forgetting Balzac, what came out of his pen was pure Dreiser tinctured with Spencer and evolution. He was simply telling a story much as he had seen it happen in life.... He wrote with a compassion for human suffering that was exclusive with him in America. He wrote with a tolerance for transgression that was as exclusive and as natural. His mother, if not immoral herself, had accepted immorality as a fact of life. Some of his sisters had been immoral in the eyes of the world. In his own passion for women he was amoral himself, believing that so-called immorality was not immoral at all but was necessary, wholesome and inspiring, and that the conventional morality was an enormous national fraud.

Swanberg does not know if any of these things were going through Dreiser's mind, but the detailed instances of Dreiser's earlier behavior have been so persuasive that it is natural for the reader to accede to this kind of climactic and cumulative passage. To cite passages in the novel itself that amount to what Swanberg says would have the effect of fragmenting his narrative, calling a halt to it in favor of addressing a text—which no matter how smoothly it is done cannot quite rectify the damage that is done to story values.

Swanberg's background as an editor and free-lance writer may have some bearing on his approach to biography. He is not an academic, and he does not have the academic's respect for texts. He does not operate on the imperative of subordinating himself to a text, thinking of himself as the student of a style. He edits his biographies to establish his voice, and it is through his voice that the portrayal of the "whole man" emerges. Even when he directly speaks of Dreiser's habits of style and of composition, there is no corresponding text by which to judge Swanberg's observations—in part, because he also does not have the academic's duty to prove his points. Thus Dreiser's literary manner is evoked but not demonstrated:

> the script [of *Jenny Gerhardt*] was indeed repetitive and overlong—a chronic failing of Dreiser and one he would never overcome. He wrote too fast, sometimes many thousands of words a day. He became engrossed in the mass, losing sight of detail. He was egocentric in writing as he was in love, thinking less of the reader than of his own need to relate and describe, careless of diction, unselective, pushed on by impatience to get at the next chapter and the next, looking always ahead and seldom back. His writing mirrored the man—a lack of taste combined with nervousness, insecurity and his actual fear of time.

"His writing mirrored the man," the biographer concludes, without feeling the need to quote the writing. Instead, it is the rhythms of Swanberg's own prose that carry the reader—the three short sentences of the above passage followed by the longer, somewhat breathless sentence that conveys a feeling for how Dreiser got caught up in his own work while being oblivious of the cost to others.

This kind of biographical writing is ultimately its own justification. It has its own literary quality, weighing and balancing Dreiser's "lack of taste combined with nervousness" against his "actual fear of time." Such prose is a compression of much archival evidence; it suggests the dimensions and proportions of the literary figures; and it speaks for itself. It is the biographer's warrant for speaking in his own voice.

Neither in his work nor in his life was Dreiser ever quite able to encompass his contradictions, which Swanberg skillfully sets out in a paragraph that would have been quite beyond his subject's ability to write:

> Pushed one way and another by emotion, he was alternately a cynic and a believer, admiring ruthless capitalists but indignant at their exploitation of the masses, shocked by man's depravity and inspired by his goodness, wishing to be a spectator and yet to reform the world, worshiping science but seeing an omen in the "kindly little Jew" [who always seemed to appear at momentous occasions in his life].

This is the scope of a life that is beyond any of its individual works, Swanberg implies.

Dreiser is an unusual achievement for a biographer who has not again taken up a writer. Swanberg sensed that as a character, Dreiser was not so different from the figures of his other biographies. In later biographies, such as *Luce and His Empire*, Swanberg pursues the same approach: the painstaking building up of a personality whose contradictions are a part of his age. As much of a propagandist as he was a newsman, Luce presumed his magazines reported the truth and had his correspondents dispatches rewritten when they departed from the company line. Like Dreiser, he apparently never confronted the discrepancy between his powerful will to shape a vision of the world and his pretensions to reporting things as they actually were.

It would be a mistake for literary biographers not to consider the example of W. A. Swanberg, for he has shown how a biography of a literary figure may through indirectly treating the subject's writing actually achieve certain literary effects sometimes absent from more academic and critical biographies. Literary values certainly inform Swanberg's style. The shape of his prose and the structure of his narratives are impeccable. His example suggests that in some cases, it may be wiser not to treat a certain text in detail—no matter how important—in order to be faithful to biography as a literary form.

The question of audience is crucial here. Swanberg does not write for specialists and does not assume his readers have much knowledge of his subject. His comprehensive command of data also ensures that not even Dreiser scholars will be familiar with the way in which the material is presented. An approach that relied on the literary criticism of others, or on Swanberg's own potting of plots or criticism, would surely have yielded a pedestrian biography. Instead, *Dreiser* is a biography written primarily as a literary work in its own right that does not rely upon other texts.

Even for literary biographers who reject Swanberg's mode, there is a lesson: a biography must have a voice which is greater than the sum of evidence that has produced that voice. In the end, Swanberg speaks for a Dreiser who is the biographer's creation. In *Dreiser*, the novelist is not just the man who wrote the books, but also the man who is himself the subject of a book.

LITERARY FIGURES

Lillian Hellman (1905–1984)

Lillian Hellman was born in New Orleans, Louisiana, the daughter of Max Hellman, a shoe salesman, and Julia Newhouse. Following the failure of Max Hellman's shoe business, the family moved to New York City, where five-year-old Lillian attended school. Her studies, however, were constantly interrupted by trips to New Orleans (for six month intervals) as her father, a traveling salesman, attended to business. Hellman describes the disconcerting impact of her bifurcated childhood in her memoir, *An Unfinished Woman* (1969). She suggests her temperamental, impatient character was formed by her different experiences in the North and the South and exacerbated by the fact that her mother's family was wealthy. This group of shrewd bankers and businessmen—described in *An Unfinished Woman* and *Pentimento* (1972)—appealed to Hellman because of their power over other people, but the ruthless Newhouses also disgusted her, and later became the basis of two of her most successful plays, *The Little Foxes* (1939) and *Another Part of the Forest* (1947), which portrayed the rapacious careers of the Hubbards in the post Civil War South.

In 1922 and 1923 Hellman attended classes at the Washington Square Branch of New York University and summer sessions at Columbia University. A desultory student, she considered a writing career, proposing to write biographies of Dante and Lewis Carroll, but she left college in her junior year for a job at the New York City publisher, Liveright, in the autumn of 1924. Although this should have been an exciting opportunity for a young woman at a time when Liveright was publishing some of America's most distinguished authors, Hellman quickly became bored with her low level assignments and proved to be an unreliable worker. At Liveright, she met Arthur Kober, a struggling writer. Facing an unwanted pregnancy, she submitted to an abortion, Kober married her six months later on December 21, 1925.

The next five years were a restless period for Hellman. While her husband established himself as a short story writer and playwright, she tried to write fiction, producing short stories of uneven quality and abandoning her attempt at a novel. The couple lived in Paris for four months, returned to the United States, and Hellman took on various jobs, including stints as a publicist and reader of plays for a theatrical agent, and as a book reviewer for the *New York Herald Tribune*.

On her own in the summer of 1929, Hellman traveled to Germany, studying at the university in Bonn, and experiencing the kind of anti-Semitism that she would dramatize in her plays, *Watch on the Rhine* (1941) and *The Searching Wind* (1944).

By the fall of 1930, when Hellman joined her husband in Hollywood, where he was employed writing movie scripts, their marriage seemed tenuous. Hellman had been involved in at least one love affair in New York City, and she was upset by her uncertain status in Hollywood—the wife of a screenwriter who got her a job at MGM reading and summarizing books for scenarios. A gentle and considerate man, Kober was patient with his wife but did not know how to help her find her forte.

Casting about for some way to renew herself, Hellman saw her opportunity in a liaison with the handsome and successful detective story writer, Dashiell Hammett. Well known as a prodigious drinker and womanizer, Hammett seemed charmed and intrigued by the aggressive Hellman, a stylish, articulate woman who wanted to write but did not know what her subject should be. Noting her dramatic flair, he suggested she write a play based on the case of two teachers in nineteenth-century Edinburgh who had been accused of lesbianism.

The story appealed to Hellman's melodramatic imagination. Through several drafts of the play, *The Children's Hour* (1934), she fashioned an account of two teachers, Karen and Martha, who successfully set up their own school only to be brought down by a malevolent child, Mary, who refuses to be disciplined and who strikes back by suggesting to her grandmother, a powerful member of the community, that her teachers have an "unnatural" love for each other. An enormous success (the play ran for over seven hundred performances on Broadway), *The Children's Hour* established Hellman as a promising playwright with a keen eye for both individual and social psychology, striking a balance between the blindness of the teachers to their own feelings and the equally blind hysteria of society, which tends to take the word of authority figures and to be swayed by the emotional impact of an accusation that cannot be overcome by the rational objections of society's sanest members—such as Dr. Joseph Cardin who tries to expose Mary's manipulative attack on Karen and Martha.'

The play also dramatizes a love triangle: both Martha and Joseph Cardin are in love with Karen, and Cardin—in spite of his defense of them—cannot entirely allay his suspicion that perhaps Karen is in love with Martha. Variations on this triangle would appear in much of Hellman's theatrical writing, in her film scripts, in her memoirs, and in her private life, for she would continue to involve herself in triangles (not divorcing Kober until 1932) and later having an affair with the publisher Ralph Ingersoll while maintaining her relationship with Hammett.

Hellman's success as a playwright brought an offer from producer Samuel Goldwyn to write screenplays. Throughout the 1930s Hellman worked for Goldwyn, creating superior scripts for her version of *The Children's Hour*, retitled *These Three* (1936) and *Dead End* (1937) as well as working in collaboration on other projects. She had unusual creative control over her own scripts and a reputation in Hollywood for independence, influenced by Hammett's radical views but acting as her own person. She was instrumental in forming the screenwriter's guild and became involved in leftist politics, briefly becoming a Communist Party member (1938–1940). She would later find it necessary to defend herself against charges of Stalinism in *Scoundrel Time* (1976).

After the disastrous failure of her second play, *Days to Come* (1936), in which she lost control of her story of a strike in a Midwestern factory town, meandering between its psychological and political implications, she regained her form in *The Little Foxes* (1939), a classic of the American theater, set in the South just after the Civil War. Her main character, Regina, holds her own with her brothers, Ben and Oscar, in capitalizing on the family business. Although the play is susceptible to a political reading, and can be analyzed as a critique of capitalism, it is equally the story of a family, each member struggling for dominance and individuality. One of the most striking features of this play is its lack of sentimentality, a hardheadedness Hellman herself exemplified in the pursuit of her career.

Until his death in 1961, Hammett was at Hellman's side, proffering advice on her scripts, though not always living with her—as Hellman admits in terming theirs an on again off again relationship. Hammett's philandering, his terrible drinking, his service in World War II, meant separations and estrangements Hellman abided, never dropping Hammett, but at the same time feeling free to engage in love affairs and to maintain her own residences.

A staunch supporter of the Soviet Union, which seemed to offer the hope that socialism might eventually lead to a truly egalitarian society free of ethnic strife and economic imbalances, Hellman initially defended Stalin's pact with Hitler in 1940, though by the writing of her next play, *Watch on the Rhine* (1941), she had seen the necessity of the United States entering World War II before Hitler abrogated the pact by invading the Soviet Union. Like *The Searching Wind* (1944), *Watch on the Rhine* focuses on the innocence of Americans and their blindness to the appeasement of fascism that had gone on throughout the 1930s. In Kurt Muller, a German anti-fascist fighter seeking momentary refuge in America, Hellman creates a vulnerable hero, a fragile man with broken hands who is constrained to strangle a foreign national who threatens to reveal Kurt's presence and to expose the network of anti-fascist groups Kurt supports. That Fanny Farrelly, the mother of Kurt's American wife, Sarah, must condone this killing in her own household and allow Kurt to escape, accomplishes Hellman's aim in bringing home to Americans the fact that they are implicated in the world's evils and must take some responsibility for combating them, even at the price of losing their innocence.

Although Hellman managed to complete a second successful play on the Hubbards, *Another Part of the Forest* (1947), she began to sense that her resources as a playwright were diminishing. Her final plays, *The Autumn Garden* (1951), *Toys in the Attic* (1960), and an adaptation of a novel, *My Mother, My Father, and Me* (1963) show that she was moving toward the form of the memoir more flexible and more open than her tightly wound melodramas.

The Lark (1955), a crisp adaptation of Jean Anouilh's play about Joan of Arc, was a great success, but *Candide* (1957), written with Leonard Bernstein, Richard Wilbur, and others, was not, and Hellman found herself tiring of the collaborative efforts required of a playwright.

She had also begun a teaching career at several universities in the 1960s, sometimes conducting classes on playwriting but just as often assigning fiction and poetry. Called on to explain her career in numerous interviews, energized by contentious campus life of the 1960s, and disgusted by the terrible failure of *My Mother, My Father, and Me*, it seemed incumbent on Hellman to present some record of herself, explaining not only the origins of her character but also revealing to a later generation what it was like growing up in the 1920s, making her way among the writers and the politics of the 1930s and 1940s, and coping with her blacklisting in the 1950s for her leftist sympathies.

Hellman's first two volumes of memoirs, *An Unfinished Woman* (1969) and *Pentimento* (1972), were an enormous success, garnering her the best reviews of her life. She became a cult figure, lionized by young people, especially women, who saw in her a role model who had held her own in a man's world while remaining feminine. There was criticism of her long term relationship with Hammett—some women viewing Hellman as the subordinate partner—but on the whole she was praised for confronting the temper of her times with magnificent courage and candor. The style of the memoirs, particularly *Pentimento*, was much admired, for her chapters read like short stories, especially her account of her childhood friend, Julia, who had become part of the anti-fascist underground in Europe and whom Hellman had aided at considerable risk to herself.

When Hellman's third memoir, *Scoundrel Time* (1976), appeared, it was initially greeted with rave reviews. Eventually, however, the tide turned as her enemies of the 1930s and 1940s' emerged to dispute her accounts. In *The Paris Review* (1981), Martha Gellhorn, Ernest Hemingway's third wife, ridiculed the contradictions and inaccuracies of *An Unfinished Woman* and made a compelling case for Hellman's having lied about many incidents to aggrandize her own life. Other attacks followed, pointing up the self-serving quality of *Scoundrel Time* and its deficiencies as history. The culmination of this criticism came in Mary McCarthy's allegation on national television that every word Hellman wrote was a lie.

Hellman received little sympathy when she decided to sue McCarthy for libel. Having built her reputation on candor, the likelihood that the stories in *Pentimento*, especially Julia's, were fiction came as devastating news to Hellman's readers, and Hellman did not deign to reply to the charges. When she died on June 30, 1984 the suit against McCarthy was still pending, but Hellman's reputation had been significantly damaged.

Yet the events of Hellman's last years should not overshadow her importance as an American playwright—one of the best this country has produced. Several of Hellman's plays—*The Children's Hour, The Little Foxes, Another Part of the Forest, The Autumn Garden, and Toys in the Attic*—are regularly revived and are likely to remain a part of the American repertory. The quality of her writing in her memoirs is high, although their final place in the canon of American literature remains to be determined, as does the precise nature of her political views, and the extent to which those views must be considered in an analysis of her writing.

Bibliography

The most important collection of Hellman's papers is housed in the Harry Ransom Humanities Research Center, University of Texas at Austin. Other significant collections of Hellman's correspondence and manuscripts can be found in Special Collections, The New York Public Library; the Billy Rose Theatre Collection, Lincoln Center Library for the Performing Arts, The New York Public Library; Special Collections, Mugar Memorial Library, Boston University; the Wisconsin Center for Film and Theater Research, the University of Wisconsin, Madison, Wisconsin; the Library of Congress, Washington, D.C.; the University of Southern California Library, Los Angeles, California; the Academy of Motion Picture Arts and Sciences, Beverly Hills, California.

Two full-length biographies of Hellman have appeared: William Wright, *Lillian Hellman, The Image, The Woman* (1986) and Carl Rollyson, *Lillian Hellman: Her Legend and Her Legacy* (1988). Wright provides a solid overview of her life, but with the exception of *The Little Foxes* does not deal in any depth with her playwriting, and he largely ignores her screenwriting. Rollyson presents a critical biography, describing the development of all of Hellman's writing, and he provides extensive new material on Hellman's politics. Both biographies are based on important interviews; Rollyson works from a much broader grasp of the archival sources. Robert Newman, *Cold War Romance: John Melby and Lillian Hellman* (1988) is an important contribution to an understanding of Hellman's politics and her personal life, concentrating on her relationship with Melby, an American foreign service officer dismissed from his position in the 1950s because of his love affair with Hellman. Peter Feibleman, *Lilly* (1988), is an effective memoir of his close association with Hellman.

Jack London (1876–1916)

One of the main exponents of American literary naturalism, a popular writer of adventure stories, a crusading journalist, socialist, and political novelist, London pioneered the role of the twentieth-century activist writer.

Jack London spent his early life around the Oakland, California docks and the San Francisco waterfront. His family was poor and life was a grim struggle—facts he later used in autobiographical novels such as *Martin Eden* (1909), the story of how a young, poorly educated man teaches himself to become a writer through dogged persistence and ruthless ambition. Born illegitimate, London identified with the downtrodden and the outcasts of society. His father, William Henry Chaney, was a traveling astrologer. When his mother, Flora Wellman, a spiritualist, married his stepfather, John London, a farmer, he took his stepfather's name.

John London's farm failed, and the family faced a continual financial struggle. His stepson, bright and energetic—later photographs reveal a vigorous, ruggedly handsome man—had an intermittent education, which ceased with grammar school at the age of fourteen (except for a few months at the University of California, Berkeley in 1897). At ten, Jack London was already working, selling newspapers and laboring as a pin boy in a bowling alley. At fourteen, he found a job in a cannery. At sixteen, like his fictional heroes, he showed independence and pluck, pitching in with his pals to buy an oyster boat. He became known as an "oyster pirate." At seventeen, he became a sailor employed on a sealing boat that took him to Japan. At eighteen, he turned hobo and toured America and Canada.

By 1895, London had embarked on a fierce program of self-education, reading Darwin, Marx, and Nietzsche. These three intellectual mentors imbued London with a vision of society as a struggle in which the fittest survived. But even the very strong could be crushed, given the political structure of society, and the true nature of a human being might not be revealed except in the struggle against nature that makes London's tales of adventure so stirring and challenging.

At twenty-one, London followed the gold rush to the Klondike, and two years later he sold his first story, "To the Man on the Trail." Soon he was producing a flood of stories and novels about the individual's quest not only for survival but for triumph over both the elements of nature and the structures of society.

Jack London's name will forever be associated with the classic story, *The Call of The Wild* (1903). It has never been out of print, and it has been translated into sixty-eight languages. The book not only made London's career as a best-selling author possible, it secured his place in American literary naturalism. The story is about a dog, Buck, half-St. Bernard and half-Scottish sheepdog. He is stolen from a comfortable California home and is brutalized as a sled dog. Nevertheless, his spirit overcomes adversity—including the challenge of a vicious dog, Spitz, and Buck earns the love of a kind Master, Thornton, to whom Buck remains loyal even after his master's death.

In *The Call of the Wild*, London put not only the suffering, adventuring, and success of his early life but also the ideas of Darwin, Marx, and Nietzsche, demonstrating how overwhelming the odds are against the individual and yet how indomitable the wild spirit in man and dog can remain. This is the hard world of American literary naturalism, which posits a universe of biological forces and societal constraints. Only individuals who are insulated by wealth and middle class comforts can escape the struggle for survival—and even then, like Buck, the comfortable bourgeois may find himself or herself suddenly thrust into the grim world that luxury can cushion but not obliterate.

The key to London's success was to make his adventure stories embody his philosophical and political ideas, rather than have those ideas explicitly drive the stories. Readers could easily imbibe London's message while apparently only reading a gripping story. For London, plot itself, the structure of the story, made his political point.

London followed up his initial success with two more short adventure novels, *The Sea Wolf* (1904) and *White Fang* (1905). In the former, it is not a dog but a wealthy literary critic, Humphrey Van Weyden, who is shipwrecked and has to contend with the ruthless Wolf Larsen, captain of a sealing schooner. Just as *The Call of the Wild* drew on London's own Klondike experience to present an authentic portrayal of a cold frontier world, so *The Sea Wolf* capitalized on London's memories of rough sea voyages. In each case, he was confronting readers with rugged and life-threatening environments in which the individual has to rely on his or her own inner resources in a way that sedate society never requires. Van Weyden, with his Dutch name, suggests that London is pointing to the intrepid spirit that had settled America but which had, in the course of several generations, become weak. In the course of his conflict with the Viking-like Larsen, van Weyden builds himself up physically and mentally, returning to society not only a stronger but much self-aware man.

White Fang reverses the plot of *The Call of the Wild*, taking a wolf-dog, brutally tamed by its first owner and trained as a ferocious attack dog, and turning it again into the wild, where it is tamed once more—but this time by a sensitive master who disciplines it to be a fearless but faithful companion. More sentimental than *The Call of the Wild*, *White Fang* presages' London's gradual deterioration as a writer. At twenty-nine, he was the most famous, the most widely read, and the wealthiest author in America. He would write increasingly for money to maintain his lavish existence of luxury homes and yachts, although he did not forsake his withering view of a harsh world where men and women had to battle both nature and society.

Like his contemporary, the great science fiction writer H. G. Wells, London was not content to use the popular genre of the adventure story to convey his analysis of society and history. Just as Wells turned to journalism and novels of social criticism, so did London, publishing novels such as *Martin Eden*, in which the hero as writer explicitly confronts the complacency of bourgeois society, finding himself at a middle class dinner table arguing for his interpretation of existence with the pillars of society, the judges and politicians who hold power and look upon the powerless as unworthy.

Other books, for instance *The Iron Heel* (1907), the story of a fascist dictatorship destroyed by socialist revolution and *War of the Classes* (1904), a collection of lectures and essays, demonstrated that London retained his commitment to social criticism. As a journalist he wrote about the Russo-Japanese War (1904) for the Hearst Papers and about Mexico for *Collier's*.

In 1902, he posed as a sailor and investigated the lives of London's East End slum dwellers, producing an exposé the next year, *The People of the Abyss*. His novel, *Smoke Bellew* (1912), covers the career of a journalist in the Yukon. Novels such as *The Valley of the Moon* (1913) drew on London's nostalgia for an agrarian life and his dislike of dehumanizing cities. It proposed an unrealistic return to the land. But increasingly his work became the prisoner of the very commercial and cutthroat civilization he deplored. And his personal deterioration—abetted by drug taking and dipsomania—is evident in his autobiographical pro-temperance novel, *John Barleycorn* (1913). *The Cruise of the Snark*, London's account of his effort to cruise the world in his schooner, is an apt example of his over-reaching. His enterprise was unrealistically ambitious and it ruined him financially. Nevertheless, his evocations of the writer as hero remain a signal achievement, and his broad and intense engagement with society still attracts generations of readers.

Jack London has had an extraordinary impact on world culture. He was avidly read in the Soviet Union, for example, and taken as the model of a progressive writer. He inspired writers such as George Orwell and Ernest Hemingway to fuse journalism and fiction, pursuing a commitment to the writing life and to literature as a way of interpreting the world. His sheer passion and output have been inspiring, even if, like his hero, Martin Eden, he committed suicide—a burnt-out case at forty.

London offered journalists and novelists a vision of the individual writer at war with the world and yet fabulously successful. He did not blink at the realities of society even as he pursued his own ambitious course. Even writers who might seem worlds apart from the aggressive, high-living London—such as the essayist and novelist Susan Sontag—have paid tribute to London's example, ignoring his excesses and honoring his quest to engage the world on his terms.

London has been equally popular, however, with readers of adventure stories, who are not devotees of Nietzsche, Marx, or Darwin. For them, it is surely London's ability to describe the world, to place readers in his characters' situations, that is so compelling. London always gives his readers a vivid sense of having been where his characters are.

As a popular writer, London fashions plots that overwhelm the seeming contradictions in his thinking. Nietzsche and Marx, for example, do not have the same vision of society or of the individual. Nietzsche would reject Marx's materialism, his emphasis on the structures of society that militate against individual success. There is no room in Marx's Communism for the superman, or superhero, as in Nietzsche. And neither Marx nor Nietzsche adopted Darwin's biological view of human beings as organisms in the evolving natural world. Yet in London, society, nature, and the individual, are synthesized in dramatic plots that defy logical analysis. London speaks simultaneously for both the social critic and the social aspirant: the individual who knows the world will crush him but who nevertheless persists in the belief that he can master his misfortunes.

Bibliography

Auerbach, Jonathan. *Male Call: Becoming Jack London* (Durham: Duke University Press, 1996). As its title suggests, this biography focuses on how London became a writer and public celebrity as well as exponent of the masculinized viewpoint that later became the forte of Ernest Hemingway.

Barltrop, Robert. *Jack London: The Man, the Writer, the Rebel* (London: The Pluto Press, 1976). A short biographical and critical study, well illustrated, with separate chapters on *The Iron Heel* and the Snark voyage, and the consequences of his fame. Includes Notes, a bibliography, and index.

Doctorow, E. L. *Jack London, Hemingway, and the Constitution: Selected Essays* (New York: Random House, 1993). A long, thoughtful reflection on London's politics and fiction from the point of view of a major novelist sympathetic but also critical of London's example.

Kershaw, Jack. *Jack London: A Life* (New York: HarperCollins, 1997). A comprehensive, lively, biography. If its reveals few new facts, it retells the story of London's life and career in intimate, revealing details.

Lober, Earle. *Jack London, Revised Edition* (New York: Twayne, 1994. A useful introduction to London which includes a chronology, notes, and annotated bibliography.

Perry, John. *Jack London: An American Myth* (Chicago: Nelson-Hall, 1981). A detailed biography, especially good on London's early life and his later adventures as sailor and journalist. Lacks illustrations but includes notes, bibliography, and index.

Sinclair, Andrew. *Jack: A Biography of Jack London* (New York: Harper and Row, 1977). A comprehensive biography, including chapters on London's period in Mexico and his later reputation. Includes excellent illustrations, notes, bibliography, and index.

Tavernier-Courbin, Jacqueline, ed. *Critical Essays on Jack London* (Boston: G. K. Hall, 1983). Contains a helpful introduction, essays ranging on many aspects of London's life and work, and a bibliography.

PHILOSOPHERS AND CRITICS

Leo Strauss (1899–1973)

A renowned political philosopher, Strauss searched the texts of both the ancients and the moderns to construct his vision of a viable politics that included the rule of the wise.

Leo Strauss was born into an orthodox Jewish family in Kirchhain Hessen, Germany, on September 20, 1899. He received a classical education in a German gymnasium and also served in the German army. By seventeen, he was a firm believer in Zionism, the belief that a Jewish homeland should be established in Palestine. His later writings include discussions of Jewish history, philosophy and culture. He studied philosophy and natural science at the universities of Marburg, Frankfurt, Berlin, and Hamburg, where he earned his Ph.D. in 1921.

Strauss studied with Edmund Husserl (1859–1938), the founder of phenomenology, an extremely influential philosophy built on the premise that there could be a science of phenomena. Husserl argued that the philosopher could develop a system describing phenomena, a system that would be as rigorous as the natural sciences. Strauss's other important teacher, Martin Heidegger (1889–1976), one of Husserl's students, rejected phenomenology to concentrate on a study of being, the human awareness of existing in time (temporality) and on how this awareness influences the human personality and its consciousness of death. These two thinkers stimulated Strauss to develop a philosophy treating politics as phenomena that could be accurately described while acknowledging politics as also subject to temporality; that is, to a historical process that kept changing the significance of politics.

In 1932, Strauss won a Rockefeller grant to study in Paris, where he concentrated on medieval Jewish and Islamic philosophy. After 1933, when Hitler took power in Germany, it became impossible for Strauss to return to Germany, and in 1937, he migrated to the United States, taking a position as a research fellow at Columbia University in 1937 and then the next year at The New School for Social Research. In 1949, he began teaching political philosophy at the University of Chicago, where he embarked on the works of his mature career.

Following Husserl, Strauss emphasized the idea of the "whole"—a term he would employ in several of his books. In order to acquire knowledge, the thinker had to have a sense of the whole—that any particular idea was related to a body of ideas and that those ideas made sense only because of their connection to a whole. By the same token, the thinker could only have an awareness of the whole by examining particular ideas. Sometimes called the hermeneutical circle (a circle because interpretation or hermeneutics constantly shift from part-to-whole and whole-to-part), this concept became valuable to Strauss as he tried to show that good government was not a historical phenomenon but a set of ideas developed by the ancient Greeks and others, a set of ideas that could be obscured by historical developments, but also a set of ideas that could be recovered by the persistent thinker and commentator on the classic texts of political philosophy.

In his early career, Strauss focused on theology, exploring the thinking of Thomas Hobbes (1588–1679) and Benedict de Spinoza (1632–1677), two philosophers who attacked traditional religion and many of the traditional explanations for the foundations of political states. Like these philosophers, Strauss explores the meanings of reason and revelation because he sees the conflict between religion and philosophy as the core of western civilization that contributed to its dynamism.

The late Allen Bloom, a professor at the University of Chicago and a disciple of Strauss, divides Strauss's career into three phases. In the first, Strauss produced two major books, *Spinoza's Critique of Religion* (1930) and *The Political Philosophy of Hobbes* (1936). He began to explore what later became his mature program of study: how to interpret the fundamental tension between the need to set up a civilized state and the philosopher's often corrosive explorations of truths that could undermine belief in the civilized state.

Strauss contended that the state rested on "noble fictions" about its founding—that it arose out of a gift of the gods or otherwise had a divine sanction. In fact, the state often resorted to violence and other forms of compulsion in order to establish and to maintain its existence. No state, Strauss believes, could survive without employing coercive means. Thinkers who had come into conflict with the state, or who had openly exposed the state's suspect substructure, could expect to be punished. Noting how philosophers like Socrates and Spinoza had been persecuted and even put to death because of their unorthodox ideas, Strauss sought a method of commentary on these thinkers and on others which emphasized the need for both exoteric (explicit) and esoteric (implicit) teaching to safeguard both the philosopher, whose wisdom could guide the state, and the state, which could profit from such wisdom only indirectly and gradually.

In his second phase, Strauss began to elaborate what he meant by exoteric and esoteric philosophy. Examining the texts of great philosophers he found passages that seemed deliberately obscure, as if certain philosophers were putting up obstacles to an easy grasp of their ideas. Since a writer like John Locke (1632–1704) was perfectly capable of writing plainly, there must be a reason for his abstruse passages. Strauss suggested that Locke wrote on different levels for different audiences. Ideas that were not controversial or that could be readily absorbed and accepted were stated directly. But ideas that might jeopardize the philosopher's authority or the authority of the state were couched in much more subtle and even elusive language and were meant only for thinkers who could approach the philosopher's own sophistication. In this sense, philosophy's meanings are hidden; they are there, in the text, but they have to be dug out and analyzed by a persistent commentator. As Bloom argues, Strauss began, in this second phase, to adopt the two-tier method he analyzed in philosophers—using an accessible style for unobjectionable ideas and an evasive style for his more challenging arguments. Regardless of historical period, Strauss found philosophers engaging in the same maneuvers of both courting and eluding their readers. As the titles from this phase suggests, Strauss (under the shadow of Hitler) was acutely conscious of writing in a world full of danger for philosophers: *Persecution and the Art of Writing* (1952), *Natural Right and History* (1953), *On Tyranny* (1963).

In his third phase, Strauss began to expand his own use of the exoteric/esoteric method. Reviewers were often baffled by his books because they did not obey the rules of conventional scholarship, which demanded that the scholar be explicit about his ideas. On the contrary, Strauss seemed to be concealed in his commentaries on the great philosophers, daring the enterprising, resolute reader to understand him just as Strauss believed the philosophers he wrote about challenged him. Even Straussians like Bloom, however, confess that they find certain of Strauss's books from this period difficult to comprehend, especially titles such as *Thoughts on Machiavelli* (1958), *City and Man* (1964) *Argument and Action of Plato's Laws* (1975).

A consistent theme in all of Strauss's work is his attack on the modern social sciences. He decried the dominant methods of academic sociologists and political scientists who tried to describe society and politics in value-neutral terms. Their moral relativism and refusal to make judgments appalled Strauss, who saw this intellectual stance as a dereliction of the thinker's responsibility. There was a wisdom of the ages that social scientists should be drawing upon and using to assess the contemporary world. To the argument that different societies had different standards and should not be assessed in absolutist terms, Strauss replied that societies might differ as to the nature of the summum bonum—Aristotle's term for the supreme good—but that did not mean that there was no such thing. Thinkers should always argue for what they saw as the truth, even if there was a dispute about what that truth was.

Strauss's influence on his colleagues and students grew steadily in nearly twenty years of teaching at the University of Chicago. When he retired in 1968, he taught briefly in California at Claremont Men's College, and then spent his remaining years as a Scholar-in-residence at St. John's College in Annapolis, Maryland, a fitting destination because of the school's emphasis on the great books curriculum, an even more rigorous education in the classics of philosophy than the University of Chicago provided. When he died, he was the recipient of lavish tributes, many of them printed in the conservative weekly magazine, *National Review*

As Shadia Drury observes in her study of Strauss, his reputation has grown considerably since his death. Reviewers often mistook the aims of his books, and in his own lifetime he was regarded primarily as an historian of ideas, and not as a philosopher.

For he seemed to subordinate himself to the texts he expounded, and he preferred to call his writing teaching. In other words, Strauss did not make any claims to being an original philosopher. Yet Drury (not a Strauss disciple) and many others treat him as an innovative, unconventional figure whom contemporary philosophy is just beginning to understand and to assimilate.

Drury and others have argued that Strauss's indirect presentation of ideas was not only deliberate; it was in itself a demonstration of his belief that philosophers cannot enunciate their most inflammatory and unorthodox ideas openly. On the contrary, philosophy must proceed obliquely—in a sense politically. Political philosophy is not just about politics; it is itself a part of politics and must proceed in a political fashion. The concrete result is that philosophers must be acutely aware of their audience, of how much their audience can absorb, and of how to advise the state and its leaders without undermining their authority.

Although the nature and significance of Strauss's ideas have been subject to many different interpretations, it is uncontestable that he is regarded as the inspiration for several generations of conservatives. Many of them, like Bloom, began as Strauss's students. Others have become political advisors to conservative administrations, following Strauss's view that philosophers can become indispensable advisors to rulers if not the rulers themselves.

Plato's idea of the philosopher-king, and Machiavelli's idea of the philosopher as advisor to the prince, inform much of Strauss's view of philosophy and philosophy's role in the modern political state. He is "conservative" in the sense that he believes his fundamental ideas derive from the teachings of the Greeks and the Hebrews, and that modern philosophy's role is to rediscover the truths of the ancients.

Strauss believes there are universal ideas, and he has a vision of politics that transcends individual cultures. He does not deny cultural differences, or that history shapes the thinker's understanding of universals, but the fact that interpretations may clash and societies may implement universals in contradictory fashions, does not destroy the idea of universals. It is in this sense that he is conservative. Conservatives have taken him as a mentor because he believes in a tradition that must be recovered and maintained against what has been called "historicism," the doctrine that ideas grow out and are changed by history, and that no idea can be said to be permanent, but rather all ideas are the product of their time and place. As a conservative and anti-historicist, Strauss has become the leading light for conservatives and others who wish to examine and perhaps even to slow down the momentum of political change.

Bibliography

Bloom, Allan. "Leo Strauss: September 20, 1899–October 18, 1973." *Political Theory* 2 (November, 1974): 372–392. An often cited intellectual biography by one of Strauss's students and colleagues at the University of Chicago.

Deutsch, Kenneth L. and Walter Nicgorski, eds. *Leo Strauss: Political Philosopher and Jewish Thinker.* (Lanham, MD: Rowman & Littlefield, 1994). Includes and excellent introduction to Strauss's life and work, along with essays on his major books and his influence on other thinkers.

Drury, Shadia. *The Political Ideas of Leo Strauss.* (New York: St. Martin's Press, 1988). Contains an excellent biographical/critical introduction and chapters on Strauss as teacher and philosopher; on his theology; on his interpretations of Socrates, Machiavelli, Hobbes, Plato, and Nietzsche; and on modernity. Concludes with a critique of Strauss's ideas. Notes, annotated bibliography, and index.

Hippolyte Taine (1828–1893)

As a critic and historian of the arts and society, HippolyteTaine dominated much of the intellectual life in France in the last half of the nineteenth century. Influential in England and America as well, much of his history and literary theory has fallen into disrepute in this century, yet his method and his appreciation of literary works continue to engage critics and historians.

Taine was twelve years old when his father, an established attorney, died. Left with a modest inheritance and scholarly inclinations, the young man was sent to a boarding school in Paris. He loved learning and soon revealed a mind superior to both his fellow students and his teachers. Deeply influenced by the philosopher Baruch Spinoza (1632–1677), Taine had lost his religious faith by the age of fifteen. He took a naturalistic view of the world, in which the human intellect and nature are viewed as parts of a single process. History, if it was examined carefully, revealed a total structure that functioned on the same principles as nature. Consequently, societies grew and declined in an organic manner just like natural phenomena, and the historian or philosopher could find the laws of society, of history, of literature, or of any human endeavor, in the same way that scientists found such laws to operate in nature.

It was Taine's devotion to Spinoza that led to his failing the "aggregation" (a series of examinations at the Ecole Normale Superieure) in 1851. His conservative examiners found his elucidation of Spinoza's moral system "absurd," according to Leo Weinstein, the author of one of the few studies on Taine available in English. In effect, Taine was flouting their most fundamental conceptions about free will and morality, for he argued that human beings were largely the products of their race, their time, and their environment. Taine seemed to attack the concept of individuality and of moral responsibility, apparently abandoning the notion that human beings created their own world in favor of a belief in determinism.

If Taine's early academic career was hampered by his unorthodox views, his lectures on literature and art soon brought him attention both in France and abroad. For he was the harbinger of the great naturalistic novelists of the nineteenth century like Emile Zola (1840–1902), who took as their subject matter the way a culture shapes human character. Taine was one of the first men of letters to study science rigorously and to develop a human psychology based on his courses in physiology, botany, zoology, and anatomy. His work was greeted with enormous enthusiasm since it promised to put the study of history, of literature, and of culture as a whole on an objective basis and free it from the arbitrary prejudices of the critic.

The publication of Taine's *History of English Literature* in 1864 solidified his reputation as the leading philosophical critic of his age. Rather than simply present summary accounts of the great English authors' lives and works, he propounded the notion that English literary history was not just the record of individual achievements. Rather it had a shape and a structure that could be elucidated, so that each author became a part of a tradition and could be seen as the product of his environment and his age. Literature was no more an accident, or merely the manifestation of an individual mind, than were the elements of nature.

In collections of essays and lectures in the next ten years and in his travels across Europe, Taine promoted a methodology based, he believed, on the rigor of scientific principles. In a lecture on the nature of art (first given in Paris in 1864 and published in English translation in 1875), Taine set out the rules of his method. First study the artist's body of work. Get to know his characteristic themes and techniques. Then examine the artistic tradition out of which he develops, taking note of how his work is illustrative of that tradition. Finally, explore the social climate, intellectual influences, the race, the language, and the customs of the world the artist inhabits. Taken in total, this method, in Taine's view, yields a comprehensive, unbiased view of art.

Taine's view of art is historical: "arts appear and disappear along with certain accompanying social and intellectual conditions," he asserts in his lecture on the nature of art. The implication of his argument is that artistic genius is an intensified example of environmental influences. The artist is the finest expression of the whole culture but not a creation unto himself. All of what makes Shakespeare distinctive can be found in his contemporaries, Taine argues, but only Shakespeare expresses the exquisite combination and modulation of those elements that make a great artist. Recurring to science as his guiding principle, Taine's concludes: "the productions of the human mind, like those of animated nature, can only be explained by their milieu." Such a statement, in his estimation, was a law he had discovered in his study of art not an idea he foisted upon it. He offers his readers "facts," for science "imposes no precepts, but ascertains and verifies laws."

It must be remembered that Taine was writing at a time when eminent Victorian figures like Thomas Carlyle (1795–1881) were advancing a great man theory of history. The legacy of Romanticism had been to exult in individualism and to see society coalescing about the figures of extraordinary men. On the contrary, Taine contends, a writer like Honore de Balzac (1799–1850) is great precisely because he creates a literature of characters who typify their times, their culture, and their race. Balzac's "human comedy," his series of novels on French life, are the best history of his era because he is so attuned to the way in which his characters are manifestations of their society. Similarly, Stendhal (1783–1842) repays study because he is so intimately aware of how individual psychology is linked to the history of his times. His characters are motivated by historical conditions; there is a logic to their imaginations that springs from their milieu.

In the last twenty years of his life, Taine shifted from an interest in art and philosophy to the writing of a history of contemporary France. Never deeply engaged by political issues he nevertheless felt the need (given his historical frame of mind) to discover the roots of his culture. Because he believed that societies grow organically, and thus that individuals and events are all connected to each other, he devised a multi-volume history beginning with the ancien regime (the era before the revolution) and ending in his own day.

The French Revolution bothered Taine because it seemed more like a disruption than a continuation of history. 1789 was the year France was radically changed from a society that evolved out of a tradition to a new country that set up a government according to universal, abstract principles. Taine did not believe such principles existed, except in so far as they might be seen evolving in history. His profoundly conservative cast of mind could not allow for a catastrophic event that suddenly transforms the structure of a society. In his view, such an upheaval is doomed to failure.

Taine is not nostalgic about the past. Indeed his history of France documents how badly off the people were in the twenty-five years preceding the Revolution. He does not deny the need for change, but he deplores the anarchy and violence of the Revolution. Napoleon restored order but at the cost of destroying liberty among various classes of the people. Having to deal with the failed revolutions of his own time (the upheaval of 1848, the Paris Commune of 1871) Taine was not sanguine about the way his countrymen effected change. His rather vague solution was to counsel a sympathetic understanding of the place of all classes and elements of society.

Except for his literary essays, Taine is not read much today. For one thing, his notions of science are outdated and suspect—particularly his emphasis on race which sounds uncomfortably like racism. Here is his description of the French revolutionary, Jean Paul Marta (1743–1793): "Issuing from incongruous races, born of mixed blood and tainted with serious moral commotions…" In a footnote, Taine explains that Marta's family, on his father's side, was Spanish ("long settled in Sardinia") and had abandoned Catholicism when his father "removed to Geneva where he married a woman of that city." Not disposed to favor a volatile revolutionary anyway, Taine resorts to the dubious ploy of discrediting a man who is the product of different cultures and religions. Many Americans, on this basis, would look suspect indeed, for they would foul up Taine's antique notions about the organic quality of race and environment.

This lapse in Taine's treatment of Marta reflects a more serious failing: the historian's inability to see that the vaunted objectivity of his methodology is no such thing. When Taine's history of France is examined, it is clear that it is just as subjective, just as determined by his biases as any other history would be. Taine would not have been very surprised by this judgment, since he believed human beings were the products of their times. Why should he be an exception? Yet he did fail to see the contradictions in his own methodology, that his brand of conservatism was temperamental and could not be explained just in terms of his time, place, and tradition.

As Edward T. Garage notes in his fine introduction to selections from Taine's history of France, Taine's reputation since his death has steadily declined. Yet Garage is right to suggest that subsequent critics and historians owe him an enormous debt. He did correct, for example, the excesses of Romanticism, its lionizing of the individual. He did perceive important facts about the relationship between the individual and society that naturalistic novelists explored with considerable brilliance. And nearly every critic who has covered the subjects and the periods that were at Taine's command has felt compelled to deal with his ideas—if only to refute them. Finally, Taine merits study as one of the last men of letters who tried to integrate his insights into so many different fields of study: psychology, literary criticism, esthetics, art, philosophy, and history. In an era of specialization, his work is still an admirable example of the effort to grasp intellectual life in its entirety.

Bibliography

Eustis, Alvin A. *Hippolyte Taine and the Classical Genius* (Berkeley and Los Angeles: University of California Press, 1951). A well written scholarly monograph that concentrates on Taine's debt to classical writers and scholarship. Information is presented succinctly and judiciously. The bibliography is still useful.

Kahn, Shalom J. *Science and Aesthetic Judgment: A Study in Taine's Critical Method* (London: Rutledge and Kegan Paul, 1953. An important monograph for specialists, this book will prove somewhat difficult for students not already familiar with several of Taine's texts. Nevertheless, this is an essential study of Taine's philosophy and methodology.

Garage, Edward T., ed. "Hippolyte Adolph Taine, The Origins of Contemporary France," selected chapters from a multi-volume history, *The Ancient Regime, The Revolution, The Modern Regime.* (Chicago: University of Chicago Press, 1974). Garage's long introduction provides important biographical information on Taine and a shrewd analysis of his position as an historian.

Weinstein, Leo. *Hippolyte Taine* (Boston: Twayne Publishers, 1972. A comprehensive introduction in English to Taine's life and work. Chapters on his life, his philosophy, method, and psychology, his career as a literary and art critic, and his role as an historian of France give a thorough summary and critique of Taine's achievements and influence. Notes, an annotated bibliography, and index make this an indispensable study

Wellek, Rene. A History of Modern Criticism, 1750–1950 (New Haven: Yale University Press, 1965). This is one of the most important sources for tracing the history of literary criticism and Taine's place within it. Wellek discusses the significance of Taine's *History of English Literature* and the way the critic deals with matters of style.

POLITICAL FIGURES

Winston Churchill (1874–1965)

One of England's greatest prime ministers and war leaders, and one of the twentieth century's greatest public figures, tremendously influential because of his actions and his writings.

Winston Churchill was born two months prematurely on November 30, 1874 at Blenheim Palace in Oxfordshire, England. He was the son of Lord Randolph Churchill (1849–1895), a prominent Conservative politician and a descendent of the Duke of Marlborough (1650–1722), a statesman and one of the greatest military commanders in history. Blenheim Palace was the gift of a grateful nation to the Duke of Marlborough for the first of his famous victories at Blenheim (1704) in the War of the Spanish Succession (1701–1714). Churchill grew up within this background of military glory and patriotism and always had it in mind to preserve and to enhance the grandeur of the British Empire.

Winston's mother, Jennie Jerome, was the daughter of Leonard Jerome, described as an "American freebooter" and as the "king of Wall Street." Winston adored his mother, although she shared little of her fashionable life with him. In his efforts to shape American opinion during the second World War and afterwards, he made the most of his American ancestry. He worshipped and stoutly defended his reckless, flamboyant, and self-destructive father—even writing a biography of Randolph (1906) in justification of his father's life. All of these qualities—filial piety, loyalty, pugnacity, grandiloquence, and enormous courage—were to make of Winston a unique figure in the twentieth century, for he was almost a throwback to an earlier age, more like an eighteenth century soldier statesman and man of letters than a modern politician.

Winston was educated at Harrow and Sandhurst, the latter school for the training of military officers. Right from the beginning of his career, he combined his craving for military exploits with a talent for journalism. Thus in 1895 he took a leave from the military to report on war in Cuba for London's *Daily Telegraph*. After serving in both India and South Africa he was assigned in 1899 to cover the South African War for the *Morning Post*. The story of his capture, imprisonment, and escape catapulted him to the forefront of British journalists. In these early adventures, Winston was already the man he would become as prime minister: rambunctious, intrepid, a bit of a bully, but nearly always an engaging and inspiring leader and writer. He quite literally thrived on words, with his favorite mode of composition being dictation, in which he could galvanize himself and his readers with a vibrant language that seemed inseparable from the man himself.

In his early career, Churchill went from success to success: elected to Parliament as a Conservative in 1900 and appointed undersecretary for the colonies in the cabinet of Sir Henry Campbell-Bannerman; serving as president of the Board of Trade (1908–1910) and as home secretary (1910–1911). In the latter post, he initiated important labor and pension legislation. In 1911, he became first lord of the admiralty and aggressively expanded and modernized the fleet. With the devastating failure of the Dardanelles campaign (1915) in World War I, however, he suffered not only his first major defeat but a far more serious blow: he became branded as a reckless adventurer, a loner in public life whose career might end as disastrously as his father's, whose life ended sadly in a series of illnesses and rages brought on by syphilis.

Churchill's early setback was by no means a mere misfortune. He had often acted arbitrarily and outside the boundaries of normal party and governmental conduct. Elected as a Conservative, he switched to the Liberal party, then switched back again to the Conservatives. As first lord of the admiralty, he often ran roughshod over seasoned naval officers—sometimes with cause, sometimes only for the misguided gratification of his own ego. To many of his political colleagues, therefore, Churchill was not a man to be trusted; he was out to serve only himself. Although the defeat in the Dardanelles was not exclusively Churchill's fault—indeed credible arguments can be advanced that his military plans were sound—his conspicuous touting of himself inevitably provoked the vehement reaction against him.

It became Churchill's life's work not only to rehabilitate his reputation but to fulfill his early promise and destiny: to become prime minister and supreme military leader. Churchill's talents were not ignored, but in various cabinet positions he was not allowed to get near the center of power: minister of munitions (1917); secretary of state for war and for air (1918–1921); colonial secretary (1921–1922); chancellor of the exchequer 1924–1929). None of these offices could call on Churchill's broad based talent for mobilizing a whole nation during periods of crisis, and he lacked real interest in domestic matters. From 1929 to 1939, he had no government position. As a member of Parliament he was a steadfast anti-Communist and an early—if not always consistent—opponent of the Fascists. Yet by the time of Neville Chamberlain's "peace in our time" capitulation to Hitler at Munich in the summer of 1938, Churchill had become fixed in his country's imagination as the prophet who had foreseen Britain's involvement in the Second World War and who had demanded military preparedness. Whereas his vitriolic Empire first speeches had once seemed dangerous and ridiculous affectations belonging to an earlier age, now his evocations of moral and military grandeur spoke eloquently to a nation that needed to be aroused to fight for its own freedom.

At various points in the thirties Churchill, physically and politically, had looked like an old man. War, however, energized him. Her was sixty-six when he became prime minister in May of 1940. His appearance no longer seemed merely overweight. He now had the heft of a powerful man. There was a spring in his voice and in his step. His famous v for victory signs and his boyish grins bespoke a man who was reborn, and yet a man of years, of vast experience, equipped better than anyone else to stay the course and to excite a nation to arms. Just as he had sounded the alarm of war, so now he broadcast the call to victory. There is ample documented evidence that his public display of confidence was no sham. To be sure, he had his moments of despair, but observers of his private life testify to a man who was irrepressible, a demon for work, a demanding—sometimes unreasonable—chief executive. He drove his staff mercilessly as he drove himself. If he commanded the power of the word, the word was transformed into actions. Churchill required results and was always quick to take action even at the risk of defeat.

His task was to spur the government and the people onward.

As prime minister in time of war, Churchill's independence was a signal strength. Although a Conservative, he had never been much of a party man, and his claim to be serving the whole nation was never better supported than during the war. Although he opposed Communism and Socialism, some of his wartime measures heralded the welfare state Britain would become after the war. Loathe to grant independence to any part of the British Empire, his vigorous prosecution of the war inevitably strengthened the successful movement for a free India.

It came as something of shock for Churchill to be turned out of office at the end of the Second World War. In retrospect, however, it seems clear that the voters knew his finest hour had been during a time of military need. Now the Labour Party would set about putting into effect a postwar economy that would make good on promises of increased social security, health benefits, and other domestic improvements desperately desired by a people weary of war.

Churchill was, of course, a world figure. With Franklin Roosevelt and Josef Stalin, he helped shape the postwar world. Present at Yalta (1945) and other important wartime meetings, he shared Roosevelt's terrible responsibility in coming to some kind of terms with the victorious Red Army. Although Churchill has a reputation for having been a staunch anti-Communist, his treatment of Stalin was inconsistent. Sometimes he seems to have thought he could charm the Soviet leader into taking a moderate, peaceful view of postwar politics. Sometimes Churchill seems to have been cynical in suggesting to Stalin there was an equitable way of dividing up Europe to the satisfaction of all the wartime allies. In truth, for all his brilliance Churchill had a weak hand to play as the representative of a declining empire and perhaps thought he could make do with guile and with ingratiation.

Churchill's disappointment over the course of postwar events is readily apparent in his famous Fulton, Missouri speech (1946) in which he coined the term "Iron Curtain" to describe the brutal way Stalin had occupied and then cut Eastern and Central Europe off from the rest of the "free world." Churchill's rhetoric crystallized what many Americans and Western Europeans had not yet articulated, and his view of the menace of postwar Communism came to dominate American foreign policy—especially in the formulation of the "Containment" strategy by which American governments attempted to prevent the spread of Communism throughout the globe. Elected prime minister twice after the war (in 1951 and 1955) Churchill was not a particularly effective leader, although his august position as world statesman was unassailable.

Whatever Churchill did not win through politics or through war, he won through the word. His many books consolidated his position in history. In 1953, he won the Nobel Prize for his writing and oratory. His six-volume history of the Second World War (1948–1953), and his *A History of the English Speaking Peoples* (1956–1958), made him appear as a figure for the ages. These books are as much myth as they are history, for Churchill had no compunction about revising the past to portray his own part in it as illustriously as possible. But the books are also reflective of a great man who was able to stamp history in his own image and to make his word stand for the deed.

Bibliography

Bonham-Carter, Violet. *Winston Churchill: An Intimate Biography* (New York: Harcourt, Brace and World, 1965). A sympathetic biography by a friend who first met Churchill in 1906 and was in a position to observe his public and private behavior, his leadership in time of war and peace, and his reactions to both victory and defeat.

Brendon, Piers. *Winston Churchill* (New York: Harper and Row, 1984). A succinct, lively and colorful one-volume biography.

Churchill, Winston. *My Early Life* (London: T. Butterworth, 1940). One of Churchill's best books, written in his fluent, engaging style.

_____. *The Complete Speeches of Winston Churchill,* ed. R. R. James. (New York: Chelsea House, 1974).

Gilbert, Martin. *Winston Churchill* (London: Heinemann, 1991). A condensation of the the definitive multi-volume life begun by Winston's son, Randolph, and carried on by Gilbert. This is a minutely detailed (sometimes day by day) account of every aspect of Churchill's life and career which is partial to his own view of himself.

Taylor, A. J. P. and others. *Churchill Revised: A Critical Assessment.* New York: The Dial Press, 1969. Studies of the statesman by A. J. P. Taylor, the politician by J. H. Plumb, the military strategist by B. L. Hart, and the man by A. Storr.

Thompson, R. W. *Generallismo Churchill.* New York: Charles Scribner's Sons, 1973. A study of Churchill's skill as a military commander based on both secondary and primary sources, including interviews with his close friends and associates. Covers Churchill's "long apprenticeship" as a war leader and his overall performance in the Second World War.

Napoleon Bonaparte (1769–1821)

One of the greatest generals in history, Napoleon also made lasting contributions to the laws and civil administration of France and other lands. His darker legacy is to have developed a dictatorial rule that is the precursor of modern fascism.

Although a native of Corsica, Napoleon Bonaparte was sent to French military schools in Brienne and Paris, where he became known as "the little Corporal" because of his small stature. Commissioned to the artillery in 1785, he later took part in fighting on behalf of the French Revolution. In 1793, he was promoted to Brigadier General, but he was imprisoned the next year when the forces in power changed from the radical Jacobins to Thermidorean reactionaries intent on stopping the reign of terror that had made the Revolution turn on its own members. But he was soon released and back in favor in October, 1795, when he dispersed a Parisian mob threatening the government.

A politically helpful marriage and victories in the field, especially in northern Italy, increased Napoleon's prestige. Other spectacular victories in Egypt, coupled with a weak government at home that was overthrown in 1799, led to his elevation as first consul in the new government. A plebiscite was held confirming his enormous popularity, and by 1801 (the year in which he made peace with the Roman Catholic Church, one of the Revolution's greatest enemies) he was the supreme dictator of France.

Napoleon's remarkable early success was in part a matter of good fortune and in part the product of an unconquerable will and energy that took the maximum advantage of every political and military opportunity. Given the chaos of the revolutionary years, it is not surprising that a military man with political prowess should do so well. With France under siege and surrounded by hostile powers, Napoleon's victories could be viewed (rather romantically) as having saved the Revolution from destruction. At the same time, his own steadiness of purpose prevented warring factions from destroying the Revolution from within.

Napoleon's life's work was to keep France in the paramount position to which he had brought it in just a few short years. If France was to be secure, it had to dominate the European continent. Thus Napoleon intervened successfully in Austria, Italy, and Germany—all enemies of the Revolution. England, with its control of the sea, was a major target, but he repeatedly failed in attempts to destroy British military power in Egypt and on the European continent.

By 1804, Napoleon had himself proclaimed Emperor. What had once been a man coming from humble origins whose energies and talents had been released by Revolutionary actions now increasingly became an individual identifying his personal successes with the glory of the state. England, Austria, Russia, and Sweden formed an alliance against him, but on December 26, 1805 he overwhelmingly defeated their armies at Austerlitz. By 1808, he was master of the Continent, with only the sea power of England to thwart his imperial plans.

Although Napoleon had made significant legal reforms in France, he increasingly relied on the force of his own personality to rule. Rather than developing some kind of governmental structure that might perpetuate his rule, or forming a strong general staff that could carry through with his military plans, he relied almost exclusively on his own genius. As a tireless worker and supremely organized person, he counted on being able to switch rapidly from one issue to another or from one field of battle to another. He had a detailed grasp of both civil and military matters that was awesome, and he refused to delegate the authority that accrued from this command of the components of power.

Napoleon thought, mistakenly, that he could use members of his own family as extensions of his will. Thus he conferred the thrones of Holland and Westphalia on his brothers Louis and Jerome. He made his stepson Eugene a viceroy of Italy and his third brother Joseph king of Naples and later of Spain. Few of these familial appointments were successful, either because his relatives were incompetent or acted independently of his wishes. Yet he continued to act as though he could invent a royal line for himself, getting his marriage to Josephine (who was unable to bear his child) annulled in 1809 so that he could marry the daughter of the Austrian emperor Francis I, Marie Louise, who bore him a son.

Between 1808 and 1814, Napoleon continued to triumph in war, but at great cost to his country. A defeat he suffered in May, 1809, in a battle with the Archduke Charles at Aspern, demonstrated his vulnerability. Yet he drove his forces on, invading Russia in June, 1812, with an army of five hundred thousand men, the largest collection of troops ever mobilized in Europe. Although he made it Moscow, the Russians had devastated their own country along the route of his advance, depriving him of the sustenance of the land, and exacerbating his problems with supply lines that became overextended. With winter overtaking him, the Russians struck back, reducing his huge army to one fifth of its original size, so that he had to hasten back to Paris to prepare a defense against an invasion. When Paris fell on March 31, 1814 Napoleon abdicated and was exiled to Elba.

A much lesser man might have accepted the verdict of history. But it was a measure of the esteem Napoleon could still compel that he was able to escape and rally France once more. In his effort to reconstruct his Empire he liberalized certain features of the French constitution, but before he could truly mobilize public opinion he was forced into battle at Waterloo (June 12–18, 1815), the decisive defeat of his career. In exile on St. Helena, Napoleon assiduously built up the myth of himself as the Revolution's man, the conqueror who had meant to liberate Europe from reactionary elements.

Napoleon's impact on his time and on subsequent events has been extraordinary. First, there was his conceit that Europe could be unified under the rule of one man. Napoleon established a cult of the personality, a disturbing phenomenon that has led to the bloody rule of Josef Stalin and Adolf Hitler in the twentieth century. Hitler, in particular, suffered from delusions of grandeur that had their precedent in Napoleon. Both leaders, in fact, were bold military strategists who imagined that if only they took over the details of command the world could be shaped according to their desires. Napoleon established the model for the world historical individual who believes in the triumph of his will.

The great Marxist critic, Georg Lukacs, has argued in *The Historical Novel* (1955), that Napoleon's movement of masses of men across a continent resulted in the development of an historical consciousness in which millions of men suddenly saw their fate linked to the fate of millions of others. Even when Lukacs' Marxist bias is discounted, his evocation of Napoleon's ability to motivate millions of people takes on an inspiring and frightening aspect. For Napoleon took the idea of democracy, of popular rule, of government by the majority, and turned it into another tool of the dictator. At the height of his own popularity, at crucial periods in his career, Napoleon used plebiscites to legitimize his military and imperial ambitions.

Historians of various biases continue to argue over Napoleon's significance, for they recognize in his example a powerful lesson on personality and politics. At the beginning of his career, Napoleon was seen as the outcome of a Revolutionary movement, as the very type of man the forces of history had shaped to rule. Yet by the end of his career, large parts of Europe regarded him only as a dictator, camouflaging his tyranny in the rhetoric of the Revolution.

The comparison with Hitler is, again, apposite. There is virtually nothing in Hitler's record that can be salvaged, no vision of a united Europe worth contemplating. The difference between him and Napoleon can be gauged by imagining what would have happened if each man had been able to conquer all of Europe. Hitler's ideology was founded on excluding and exterminating various groups of people. Napoleon's ideology was based on the principle of inclusion. Armies were defeated in the field, and though civilian populations also suffered in the Napoleonic wars, the Emperor had no final solution, no master plan, to rid Europe of undesirable elements. If Napoleon did betray much of the Revolution, he also left a code of law and an enviable legacy of civil administration. He is not the monster Hitler was precisely because Napoleon did come out of the context of a Revolution, which in practice he may have subverted but which he also supported in a way that still influences scholars of his period today.

Bibliography

Cronin, Vincent. *Napoleon: An Intimate Biography* (London: Collins, 1971. As the title suggests, this biography aims to give a close up view of the man. Written in a clear, conversational style, this is by no means one of the classic works on Napoleon, but it is an accessible way of studying a figure who has been layered with so many different interpretations. The Notes and the Index sections are helpful guides to further research.

England, Steven. (New York: Scribner, 2004). One of the finest biographies of Napoleon, assessing both his personal and political lives with considerable empathy. Englund discounts the analogy between Napoleon and Hitler, seeing the former as a progressive, if greatly flawed, figure in world history.

Geyl, Pieter. *Napoleon For and Against* (London: Constable, 1944). This study by a great Dutch historian is essential reading. With great clarity and impartiality he lays out the various reactions to Napoleon that still govern writing on him today. Geyl is an acute student of nationalism and shows how nationalistic reactions to Napoleon color much of the writing that has been done on him.

Hobsbawn, E. J. *The Age of Revolution* (London: Weidenfeld and Nicholson, 1962). Napoleon cannot really be understood apart from his age. This classic history by one of the most important British historians of the century brilliantly evokes a sense of the historical period and of social and political change.

Jones, R. Ben. *Napoleon: Man and Myth* (Kent, England: Hodder and Stoughton Ltd., 1977). Should be read after consulting one of the standard biographies of Napoleon. Divided into chapters on historical background, Napoleon's civil and military career, and the impact of his myth, this is a very useful study that includes maps, bibliographies, and chronologies of important periods and events.

Lefebvre, Georges. *Napoleon 1799–1807, Napoleon 1807–1815* (London: Routledge and Kegan Paul, 1969). This is a translation of one of the greatest biographies of Napoleon. While it focuses on the man, the biography opens with a first chapter that helpfully situates him in the context of his revolutionary times.

Palmer, R. R. *The Age of Democratic Revolution* (New York: Oxford University Press, 1964). This is a particularly lucid overview of the Napoleonic period. Palmer's balanced prose and helpful bibliography are essential and should be read in conjunction with Hobsbawm's classic study.

Stendahl. (Marie Henri Beyle) *The Red and the Black* (1831). Stendahl served in Napoleon's army and was his great admirer. In this novel, his masterpiece, he traces the career of Julien Sorel, a young man of Napoleonic ambitions. There is no finer source for appreciating the power of Napoleon's myth on his generation and on the generations to follow.

Tolstoy, Leo. *War and Peace* (1862–1869). No student of Napoleon can afford to overlook this great novelist's attack on the great man theory of history. The novel is an epic view of Napoleon's invasion of Russia and of the inexorable historical forces that Tolstoy's characters finds themselves caught up in.

ARTISTS

Rembrandt (1606–1669)

Generally considered to be the greatest portrait painter of all time, Rembrandt is also renowned for his etchings and drawings.

Rembrandt van Rijn was born on July 15, 1606 in Leiden, the son of Harmen van Rijn, a miller, and Neeltgen Willemsdochter van Zuidbroeck, the daughter of a baker. After seven years in Latin School and a very brief period at the University of Leiden, he studied for three years with Jacob van Swanenburg (a pedestrian painter) and for about six months with Pieter Lastman, who influenced his treatment of mythological and religious subjects, particularly with respect to the use of vivid expressions, of lighting, and of the high gloss that appears on many of his earliest works.

Rembrandt's earliest known dated painting, "The Stoning of St. Stephen" (1625), is a work that brims with action: the saint's face is tilted up toward a central figure, who stands with a large stone raised over his head in both hands. His arms form a triangle that defines the space around the kneeling saint filled with several men, stones in hand. Their arms and twisted bodies form powerful diagonals in contrast to the saint's own outstretched, diagonally positioned arms. The vividly realized faces and the skillful composition of a large crowd (with numerous faces peering through outstretched arms) suggest Rembrandt's early mastery of both large subjects and individualized figures.

By his early twenties, Rembrandt was working in Leiden as an independent master making his living by painting portraits but also devoting considerable time to biblical and mythological subjects. He was attracted to the faces of the anonymous poor, often using them to portray philosophers and biblical characters. "Two Scholars Disputing" (1628) is a fair example of his penchant for presenting scenes that seem like a slice of life and yet are unconventional and not easily defined. There is nothing particularly symbolic or representative about the scene. It seems rather about a point of view toward life, an intimate observation of two men—one of whom is seen only from the back and side as the other focuses his eyes on him and points to a particular page in the text they are evidently arguing over. As in much of the artist's later work, there is a sense of something having been left out, of the painting concealing as much as it reveals about its subjects. They share something that is precisely what the viewer cannot recover from the painting.

The etchings Rembrandt did of himself in 1630 suggest a man of considerable humor and anger. In the 1630's Rembrandt enjoyed a happy marriage that was marred by the deaths of his first three children. By the time he had moved to Amsterdam and married Saskia van Uylenburgh (who became the model for many of his works), he had already produced great art, such as "The Anatomy Lesson of Dr. Tulip" (1632), a powerfully dramatic painting, with a poised Dr. Tulip able to command the attention and wonder of seven observers, each of whom gazes fixedly on the cadaver's forearm as the doctor proceeds, scissors in hand, to make his demonstration. As in "Two Scholars Disputing," Rembrandt accomplishes the uncanny feat of suggesting a scene has just been entered and not merely observed from the outside.

"The Presentation of Jesus in the Temple"(1631) is an early commanding example of Rembrandt's calm skill in presenting biblical subjects. As Michael Kitson suggests, this is a picture about looking—the high priest, the rabbis, the large collection of worshippers are angled in positions that emphasize their excited observation of the Christ child. What is more difficult to see in the reproduction of the painting is the smooth finish of Rembrandt's technique, the way soothing, polished color is applied to this reverent, yet epic scene. Although the temple ceiling is very high, the illumination of the central group rivets the viewer's attention.

Saskia died in 1642, leaving a tremendous void in Rembrandt's life. Yet he managed to paint a masterpiece, "The Company of Captain Frans Banning Cocq and Lieutenant Willem van Ruytenburch," more popularly known as "Night Watch" (1642)—an erroneous eighteenth-century title that was abandoned when the painting was cleaned, revealing a dramatically lit portrayal of eighteen militiamen. Rembrandt's characteristic small touches make he painting appealing: the children wandering among the armed men, the dog scampering about, the men in varying stages of readiness, checking their rifles, conferring in small groups, and in general inspecting their equipment. Utterly absent from the scene is any sort of staginess or self-conscious presentation. In its sense of depth, of shadow and light, of strong vertical, horizontal, and diagonal lines, the painting moves the eye just as these figures are moved by their preparations. Somehow Rembrandt puts his viewers in sync with the rhythms of his subjects.

What is extraordinary about such pictures is their lack of subject or theme. On the face of it, such paintings do not have any particular message to convey. They do not commemorate some specific event, and they do not invite viewers to take a specific attitude. Yet such works are authentic and intriguing, as though the figures have just stepped into the artist's frame.

In the 1640's Rembrandt turned toward religious painting—perhaps in response to the death of his wife. "The Holy Family with Angels"(1645) presents an almost homely looking, full figured Mary bending over the cradle of Jesus as Joseph works on a piece of wood in an interior scene of comforting domesticity.

Rembrandt's landscapes and etchings during this period suggest his enormous talent for evoking a place in a few strokes and with great originality, always emphasizing the individuality of scenes.

By the end of the 1640's Rembrandt took his servant, Hendrickje Stoffels, as his mistress. A clause in Saskia's will made it impossible for him to marry again, but his depictions of Hendrickje in his art rivaled his deep feelings for Saskia. Hendrickje seems to be the subject of "A Woman Bathing"(c. 1654), a lovely illustration of Rembrandt's later manner, where patches of color blend together and human faces have a shaded suggestiveness to them, an expression they seem to have for themselves when they are all alone. Such figures convey the feeling of being seen from the inside out, as though the artist is rendering their feelings and not those of an eavesdropping observer.

Similarly, "An Old Man Seated in an Armchair" (1652), has been described as one of Rembrandt's most poetic paintings, with reds, orange-browns and yellows that blend together and fracture the precise color schemes of earlier paintings. The result is a new fluidity and grace, an artful vigor that is in curious contrast with the aged man's obvious weariness as he rests his right hand against the side of his head and casts his eyes downward.

In his middle age a few years later Rembrandt was declared insolvent, his great art collection sold to satisfy his creditors. He remained a respected figure in Amsterdam but also something of a recluse who did not recover his full powers until the 1660's, when he produced some of his greatest works, including "The Syndics of the Drapers' Guild," a painting that presents a probing analysis of cloth merchants who seem to have been caught in a moment of business. They have what might be called seasoned faces—eyes, in particular, that gaze out from the painting in various guises of watchfulness and inquiry. The viewer feels the weight of their stares and senses what it must be like to do business with these formidable men.

Although Hendrickje died in 1663 and Titus (Rembrandt's only surviving child by Saskia) in 1668, the artist continued to produce great work—not the least of which were his self-portraits, begun in his youth and continued to the very year of his death. His self-portrait of 1640 presents a handsomely clothed and composed figure—obviously a successful and self-confident artist. His self-portrait of 1650 seems less open, perhaps more reserved, and the one of 1652 offers the face of man, hand on hips, toughened by experience. Later self-portraits suggest an aging but durable figure, with one (c. 1660) composed of very heavy brush strokes and a roughened texture that bespeaks the pain and weariness of his later years. There is, however, a majesty in some of these portraits—particularly in the one of 1669, where old age and experience may have given depth to the eyes but no trace of the weariness Rembrandt painted in the countenances of other old men.

In the very year that Rembrandt died he produced a self-portrait that is massive in its philosophical attitude. No portrait painter has equaled the depth and range of his work or had the technique to rival his surface polish and attention to detail. Often Rembrandt's portraits seemed to be grooved with life—a result, in part, of his using the butt end of the brush to apply paint. His touch was as bold as it was delicate, but in his own time he was faulted for picking lower class subjects and for not staying within the sublime limits of great art. More modern critics, on the other hand, have welcomed him as a contemporary, who has shown that it is not the artist's choice of subject per se but what he does with his material that is most important. Rembrandt could make a philosopher of a beggar, and he could turn a painting about businessmen into a work of art that gives the viewer a palpable sense of what it means to transact business with the painter's subjects. Rembrandt's perceptions, in other words, grow out of his subject matter, but in doing so, transcend the subjects his paintings are about. In the end, his painting—like his etchings and drawings—exists for its own sake, creating rather than merely reporting its subject matter.

Bibliography

Clark, Kenneth. *Rembrandt and the Italian Renaissance* (New York: New York University Press, 1966. An elegant study by one of the century's great art critics, this volume includes 181 black-and-white plates, a short bibliography, notes, and an excellent index.

Goldscheider, Ludwig. *Rembrandt: Paintings, Drawings, and Etchings* (London: Phaidon Press, 1960. A superb set of 128 plates, thirty-five in color, with an introduction by Goldscheider and three early biographical accounts reprinted in their entirety. Extensive notes and an index make this a very useful volume.

Haverkamp, Begemann. *Rembrandt: The Nightwatch* (Princeton: Princeton University Press, 1982. A historical and critical study of one of Rembrandt's most famous paintings. With over ninety illustrations, including a handsome fold-out color plate, this is an excellent example of scholarly thoroughness.

Kitson, Michael. *Rembrandt* (London: Phaidon, 1969). A succinct study of Rembrandt's life on art, divided in sections evaluating his art, his "subject pictures," portraits, and landscapes. An "outline biography" gives the most important dates in the artist's life and forty-eight large color plates provide a handsome and representative sampling of his work.

Rosenberg, Jakob. *Rembrandt: Life and Work* (Ithaca: Cornell University Press, 1964). A revised edition of the classic 1948 comprehensive study artist's life and work, with separate chapters on portraiture, landscape, biblical subjects, Rembrandt in his century, and style and technique. Heavily footnoted and well indexed. The bibliography is of limited usefulness since it refers mainly to untranslated European sources.

Wallace, Robert. *The World of Rembrandt 1606–1669* (New York: Time-Life Books, 1968). A very useful study of the life, the times, and the art of Rembrandt, including chapters on "The Legend and the Man," "Prelude to Greatness," "Rembrandt's Holland," and "An Exploration of Styles." A rich selection of black-and-white color plates cover all phases of the artist's career and include comparisons with the work of his contemporaries and models. A chronology of the artists of Rembrandt's era, an annotated bibliography, and index make this an essential text.

Rubens (1577–1640)

One of the most successful artists of his time, with a huge workshop of artists who completed many of his commissions, Rubens is regarded as the most important creator of Baroque art. As a distinguished diplomat he used his cheerful personality and broad human interests to work for the cause of peace.

Peter Paul Rubens was the son of a Protestant attorney from Antwerp who moved to Germany to escape religious persecution. Although Rubens was baptized a Calvinist in Germany, he became a devout convert to Catholicism. When his father died in 1587, he and his mother returned to Antwerp, where he apprenticed himself to several local painters. From his last teacher, Otto van Veen (1556–1629), he acquired considerable knowledge of Italian painting. By 1600, Rubens was in Rome, studying and copying the works of the Italian Renaissance, and preparing himself to become the first Northern European painter to combine the grandiose and realistic styles of the Italian and Dutch masters.

Very little survives from Rubens' Italian period (1600–1608), but in his "Portrait of the Marchesa Brigida Spinola-Doria" (1606) there is evidence of his early efforts to make his mark in the tradition of international portrait painting. As Jennifer Fletcher points out, the artist's subject came from a family that owned portraits by Titian (c. 1485–1576), who was renowned for his vivid color and expressiveness. The Marchesa's exalted social position is suggested by the elegance and amplitude of her luminous dress, by the crimson drapery that flows behind her in the center of the frame, and by the beautifully sculpted architectural details—all of which convey a richness and harmony of effect. What makes the painting truly remarkable, however, is its liveliness. This is no staid study of a society matron. She looks as though she is about to smile as she moves through the artist's frame. There is energy in her face, in the details of her clothing, and in the setting that makes this scene triumph over the mere reporting of details.

In 1608, Rubens returned to Antwerp but failed to reach his ailing mother in time. He planned to resume residence in Italy, but his success in Antwerp was so immediate and overwhelming (he became court painter to the Spanish viceroys of The Netherlands) and was followed quickly by his marriage in 1709 to Isabella Brant, that he never saw Italy again. His happy marriage is illustrated in a portrait of himself and his wife (1609). They are seated together in a honeysuckle bower, her hand resting gently and comfortably upon his in the center of the frame, his right foot partially underneath her flowing dress, they look out toward the viewer, forming a picture of mutual contentment and intimacy. Most striking is their sense of ease and equality. Although the artist is seated above his wife, he is also leaning toward her—any dominance he might seem to have is mitigated by the fact that his hat is cropped at the top while his wife's is shown in full, making her larger figure command the right side of the frame. When the positioning of their bodies and their clothing is compared, it is clear that Rubens has shown a couple that complements each other in every conceivable way. This dashing portrait reveals a man on the brink of a great career.

The years immediately following Rubens' return to Antwerp were vigorous and innovative. Two large triptychs, "The Elevation of the Cross" (c. 1610–1611) and "Descent from the Cross"(c. 1611–1614), altarpieces for Antwerp Cathedral, confirmed his great ability to create monumental yet realistic works of art. The fifteen foot central panels create a sense of deep space and perspective while also conveying great struggle and strain. The cross is raised by heavily muscled men in a powerful diagonal movement that bisects one central panel. Below the cross is a dog in the left hand corner sticking out its tongue in agitation while the trees in the upper right-hand corner seem to rustle in the wind. This is a painting that concentrates on the dynamism of the event whereas in the "Descent from the Cross," the limp and ravaged body of Christ is carefully taken down by his followers, with each one expressing grief in bodily postures and gestures that concentrate nearly all of the emotion of the scene on their reactions. In their bent bodies, outstretched arms and hands, grasping fingers, and intensely focused faces, the coherence of their feelings is evident. They are at one with the event.

Work on such scale demanded that the artist take on collaborators. While Rubens would work out the conception of a portrait, a landscape, a religious or mythical subject, he often left the details or some part of a painting to his pupils and collaborators. Thus in a letter referring to "Prometheus Bound" (1611–1612) Rubens notes that the eagle pecking Prometheus's liver was done by Frans Snyders (1579–1657). That these paintings are animated by Rubens' prodigious imagination is proven by his enormously powerful sketches, such as the one of a lioness (c. 1614–1615) which captures its power and grace from the rear—its huge tail sweeping through the center of the drawing and to the left, with its massive head sweeping from the center of the frame to the left, its huge paw lifted in mid stride.

Rubens was drawn to exotic subjects like a "Tigers and Lions Hunt" (1617–1618). Although his animals are anatomically correct (he studied them in the menageries of noblemen), this stirring painting is about the enormous courage of the hunters and the natural ferocity of beasts. Such paintings appealed to a Europe was still discovering foreign lands and were a form of entertainment. As C. V. Wedgwood observes, many of these paintings are still admired today for their composition and restraint, for Rubens tends to emphasize the self-control of his human figures even as they seem about to be torn apart. Rubens was a man of great energy (often rising at 4 a.m. to work), a devoted family man, a shrewd businessman, and an even tempered artist that made him invaluable as a respected emissary in the courts of Europe. Isabella, Regent of the Southern Netherlands, sent him on diplomatic missions to Spain and England, and he worked tirelessly to bring Holland back into the Spanish Catholic company of nations. Having worked as a commissioned artist all his life, he understood the importance of compromise, of balancing competing interests.

After seventeen years of happy marriage, Rubens's wife died in 1626. Four years later he married Helene Fourment, enjoying another happy marriage that is reflected in his mellow, luscious paintings of the late 1630's—for instance "The Three Graces", in which Venus and her handmaidens frolic in a dance-like rhythm, their arms enfolding each other, their flesh visibly showing the imprint of each other's fingers. Rubens paints human flesh that ripples loosely, is firm and yet plaint, and exquisitely modulated in many different tones of white, red, and brown. No other artist of his time could convey the same quality of a painting ripening into view.

In his last years, Rubens returned to landscape painting with renewed vigor. In "Landscape with a Rainbow" (c. 1635), he emphasizes an ordinary country scene—cattle, a pond with ducks, two women walking down a road past a driver and cart—in a way that suggests the daily coming and going of a rural scene, of precisely those activities which define a landscape momentarily distinguished by a rainbow. His ploy is the opposite of so many of his predecessors who use rustic settings in a stylized fashion to suggest the sublimity of nature. In "Landscape With a Sunset" (c. 1635) there is a kind of visionary quality, a perfect blending of the land, the trees, the sheep, the building at the far right edge of the painting, and the individual seated with a dog beside him against a sky turning various shades of grey, purple, and yellow. As in "Landscape with the Chateau De Steen" (c. 1635), the depiction of nature seems to be an end in itself, an evocation of harmony and balance that expresses the artist's inner nature. But the details of these scenes are so sharply realized that they never blur into vague idealizations.

Rubens died in 1640 of a heart attack that was apparently brought on by his gout, a debilitating illness that had crippled him periodically for three years. It did not stop his gigantic productivity. If there were days when he could not paint, there were other days when he probably worked faster than any other artist of his time. His lusty spirit was translated into a facility with brushwork that was truly extraordinary. The virility and sensuality of his work has been undiminished by time, though the intensity of his religious devotion may be more difficult to appreciate in a secular world not used to equating the flesh and the spirit as closely as Rubens did in his day.

Bibliography

Fletcher, Jennifer. *Rubens* (London: Phaidon Press, 1968P). An excellent introduction to the painter's life and career, discussing his diplomatic experience, society portraits, family portraits, and landscapes. Includes a bibliography and detailed notes on forty-eight full-color plates

Jaffe, Michael. *Rubens and Italy* (Ithaca: Cornell University Press, 1977; London: Phaidon Press, 1977). A comprehensive study of the influence of Italian painting on Rubens. This is a revision of a doctoral dissertation that is carefully documented but strangely organized. There is no list of plates, but after the Notes section there are indexes of works and persons that are not noted on the Contents page. The black-and-white and color plates make this an indispensable if somewhat cumbersome volume to use.

Martin, John R. *Rubens: The Antwerp Altarpieces* (New York: W. W. Norton, 1969). A thorough, copiously illustrated (in black-and-white) study of Rubens's great triptychs, "The Raising of the Cross" and "The Descent From the Cross". Martin includes an informative introduction, contemporary documents, important essays by distinguished artists, critics, biographers, and historians as well as a bibliography of books and articles.

_____. *Rubens Before 1620* (Princeton: Princeton University Press, 1972). A somewhat specialized collection of essays edited by Martin. Sixty-eight black and white illustrations and a catalogue provide helpful information on the background, the context, the shape, and the location of Rubens's early work.

Wedgwood, C. V. *The World of Rubens 1577–1640* (New York: Time-Life Books, 1976). One of the most comprehensive introductions to Rubens's life and work by one of the most distinguished historians of the seventeenth century. Covering all aspects of Rubens's life, including his years in Italy and his diplomatic career, there is no better volume to consult for a sense of Rubens's place in history. A chronology of the artists in Rubens's day, and an annotated bibliography and index, make this an indispensable study.

0-595-34181-0